THE SECRET OF BECOMING INVINCIBLE FROM POWERLESS

"SUNIL is a certified life coach and US Military veteran with Physics and Applied Mathematics educational background. He was introduced to meditation through 21 days of practice of BANGLAMUKHI Sadhana at an early age. At the age of 14, he found his Guru from whom he received TANTRA-MANTRA-YANTRA Sadhana, hypnosis, and reiki practices. Under the supervision of his Guru, he successfully completed the training in KUNDALINI AWAKENING. By the age of 14, SUNIL wrote 16 books, but due to economic hardship and family issues, only one named SPANDAN (a poem collection) was published in 2006. He taught yoga formally in 2010. Though he was born in extreme adversity, he imagined studying in the USA, and in 2011, he turned his thought into reality. He also lived his childhood dream of joining the US Army and visiting Iraq. He helped many depressed soldiers to find the purpose of their lives. All thoughts can be transformed into realities via methods, as he claims. In 2018, he tested his knowledge and techniques of attracting wealth and successfully made the desired amount, enough for buying a house with cash, from nothing in less than a couple of years. After getting out of the Army in 2020, he decided to share the techniques of transforming thoughts into realities, a yogic way, with everyone via his book 'A Mental Metamorphosis of Mind.'

His website feel-the-light.com and DHYAN-GYAN Facebook page disseminate the wisdom he received from his Gurus and almost two decades of meditation experiences in the universe." His novel 'ARKAINIST; A boy from the Sun' is getting published soon.

A MENTAL METAMORPHOSIS Of MIND

A PROVEN & YOGIC WAY OF ATTRACTING HEALTH, WEALTH, & AKASHIC RECORD

THE SECRET OF BECOMING INVINCIBLE FROM POWERLESS

SUNIL AD

A Mental Metamorphosis of Mind by Sunil AD
Published by Sunil AD
Austin, Texas, USA
feel-the-light.com

Adhikarisunil271@gmail.com
For information about special discount for bulk purchases, please contact the above email address.
Cover by Gan
ISBN: 978-1-7376341-0-2
Printed in United States of America
First Edition

This book is designed based on the author's personal experiences and intended to provide information that the author believes to be true and accurate. Though each and every exercise discussed in the book is backed up by scientific research papers from different disciplines of science, neither the author nor the publisher is offering individualized advice to any specific field such as physical exercises, diet, investment portfolio, physical health, and other mental exercises. A competent professional, trainer, or teacher should be sought for expert assistance in investment, physical exercises, and meditation. This book is not affiliated with any religion and does not intend to hurt the feelings of religious-minded individuals. If somebody feels in such a way, that is only a coincidence. The science and philosophy discussed in the book as a backup of certain principles may change over time, changing the status of the information in this book. Also, some codes and philosophies discussed in the book are solely based on the author's imagination that both the author and the publisher disclaim the responsibility for any economic loss or other possible risks of any type. Author believes that the methods discussed in the book are life-changing. However, the data, information, and results provided in the book are based on the author's and his students' experiences but no guarantee is made concerning the accuracy of the outcomes that everyone may have. The primary intention of the book is to provide information. Though the incidences mentioned in the book are real, the characters' name and addresses are fictitious. If any examples or the characters mentioned in the book resemble any living or dead, and if anybody's feelings are hurt, it is just a coincidence. The author is the editor and the producer of the book. There may be some grammatical errors or typos, or the selection of some words in the particular case may not be the best. If anyone comes across them during the exploration, readers are requested not to waste their time in emailing authors in such regard.

ACKNOWLEDGEMENTS

All that I am and will be, I owe to those books I read in my childhood because they were my friends and hope during the mental development phase of my age. I cannot stop thanking countless people who taught me several things: music, painting, poetry, and stage play. I also want to remember my friends who constantly believed in me and motivated me during my struggle times. I also like to dedicate this book to my leaders, peers, and subordinates from US Army who trusted my inner capability and supported me throughout my Army career. Basically, this book won't be possible without the instructions and motivations directly or indirectly from all intellectual people I met, including my school teachers and spiritual gurus.

WHY IS THIS BOOK WRITTEN?

Though we live in the same world, we all have created our own mental world regardless of the reality and the truth. The struggle is the reality; hunger, starvation, and miseries seem to be predetermined for most of the people. Adversity is the most substantial gravity that pulls the poor and their generation towards it forever. Besides poverty, the inferior mentality of a person plays a crucial role in determining their position in the materialistic world. The most incredible illusion of the suffering people, whether poor, sick, or depressed, is that they think they are in the worst position and have no outlet to get out. People have their own way of seeing the world, and their methods to get out of the situation depend upon the information and knowledge they acquired throughout their life. A tap connected to the water tank only gives you the water. You cannot wish to get milk out of it and get depressed when the desire is not fulfilled. Similarly, a happy person pukes out happiness through his words, and a gloomy person can turn a joyful environment into a funeral vibe. This is simply because of what we are composed of.

We are emotional beings, and always our emotions have driven the car of our life. Many of us cannot manage to take control of our own life. As a result, we become the puppet of others who are accomplished at transforming their emotions into strength. It is lucid that only 5-10 percent of the entire population rules over the rest. Only a few, minimal, poor individuals manage to climb up the ladder of wealth. Even after being successful outside in the materialistic world regardless of the sectors such as business, acting career, or the spiritual journey, the inner world of a person has to be prosperous on an emotional level. Emotions are the cause of our vibration, and thoughts or interpretations of what we perceive cause emotions. The words that we do not understand cannot make us sad, neither can involve in a thought process to create a reality. This book presents a step-by-step exercise that allows us to rebuild our inner world by working on our thoughts on the fundamental level.

A Mental Metamorphosis of Mind is written to help people change their thought processes if they are detrimental to their wellbeing. All exercises and techniques discussed in this book are 100% personally experienced and backed up by academic research papers. As I am a student of Physics and applied math, I strongly abhor superstitions. I have tried to make sense of Physics, Chemistry, Organismal biology, Psychology, Computer, Philosophy, and math to back up my claims. However, less than 5% of the information came out of my mind with no supporting shreds of evidence because they are my thoughts. The connotation of the book goes beyond the achievement of the materialistic world. Moreover, it profoundly concerns the permanent source of happiness; there must be a way to vibrate in bliss forever. You can disagree with my opinions but cannot ignore the consequences of the exercises mentioned in the book.

The most primary goal of sharing my experience is to show the world that everything is possible and our wishes can be turned into realities. Whether you want to live a prosperous materialistic life or start a monk and spiritual life, you got to be deserving for that, and this book will make you well worthy of everything and opens the door of health, wealth, and wisdom.

This book is floating on the sea of information where there are already big fishes and sharks prevailed. I hope it will survive the turmoil of the sea and reach the hand of wretched but optimistic, ignored but enthusiastic, and failed but determined people.

The Sources Of my Knowledge and Understanding:

Beyond the doubt, the human mind is an accumulation of information. Thoughts keep on racing, shaping and destroying our realities. Scientists believe a healthy mind is a platform of more than 60,000 running thoughts in a day, but where those thoughts come from? You will understand more if I give you the following analogy.

The human was created for self-governing; he is autonomous. He makes decisions based on experiences (past), and those can be of anybody. I mean, we can learn from somebody else's experiences. Our brain constantly records 24/7 without rest like a recording tool. This machine records via different sources like our five senses; eyes, ears, tongue, skin, and nose. If only one or two senses assist the brain in recording, it will access the most relevant information recorded in the past related to the most recent information fed to it. As a result, the data forms pictures, and we see them inside our heads. In this case, the chances of viewing the wrong image in mind are high. For example, if I tell you to imagine an apple that I have in my pocket, you will spontaneously imagine a red or green apple, or whichever you have seen more often. But actually, I was talking about a golden apple that is in my pocket. You could never imagine a golden apple because your brain had never recorded the info about the golden apple in the past.

The brain is a physical location of information, and the mind is the virtual world created by the data. When we talk about the imagination, we talk about the virtual world of the information we made through reading, listening, seeing, feeling, and so on. Paying attention is more crucial. Your brain may not record the info just by seeing something; you need to observe the things. Suppose you are recording your voice with a tape recorder for a singing competition, but you chose the wrong location with tons of distracting noises. The machine will also record the background sounds, and your voice won't be recognized. Similarly, the brain does the same thing; if you want the result, you have to pay close attention.

When you were a child, you had a vast open space in your memory disc. Thus, you were capable of memorizing things quickly. As you grew older, the brain keeps recording billions of information, and some of them shaped your character; some distinguished you from others. This is how and why the environment plays a vital role in moulding the nature of a child. By saying environment here, I am talking about the people around you, the sources of information around you such as books, entertainment, computers, etc. The more positive information you feed into your brain; the more optimistic thought come across your mind. This is how we are the accumulation of data.

In the 1900s, there was no cell phone, internet, or any means of communication and entertainment like today. Books were only the choice to enhance ourselves. Since I am from a working-class family, I was introduced to hard work at an early age. We had our family tea shop, a kind of small restaurant. While helping my dad with the business, I met various intellectual persons, including Ph.D. scholars and monks. I met several poets, journalists, singers, actors, and politicians. I was highly influenced by each of them. A journalist helped me publish my poem in a newspaper while I was nine, which motivated me to write more. I learned music, painting, acting, and cooking in the same way. I got opportunities of seeing, understanding, and demonstrating many skills in my childhood. Everything happened so effortlessly that I never felt like I tried hard to learn things. As the time passed, I involved myself in the reading more than going out and playing with the kids my age. When I was 12, I started hanging out with educated and accomplished people like poets, doctors, and musicians. My immature brain accumulated tremendous information from hands-on experiences and much more from the books.

I had a vast selection of genres in books; psychology, anthropology, technology, medicines, magic, history, interesting facts, self-help books on wealth, spirituality, and religion. I read Vedas, Bhagwat Geeta, Upanishads, more than ten Puranas (all Hindu scriptures). I took a Bible class in the US. I tried to understand the point of view of all major religions. From my childhood to adulthood, my time was always occupied by learning or teaching. I learned from everyone and everywhere. My thought process and imagination are based on the experiences I got from intellectual people, including my Guru, and world-changing scriptures and books. There is a vast optimistic world inside my mind. While talking about spirituality, I learned hypnosis, palmistry, astrology, reiki-healing, yoga, and pranayama (breathing technique) informally with various teachers. When I was 14, I found my Guru from whom I received the blessing on *TANTRA-MANTRA-YANTRA*, a very sacred and secret way of chanting. I studied and adhered to all eight principles of Yoga suggested by Maharshi *Patanjali*, a yogi who compiled the Yoga into a book called Yoga Sutra. My level of the meditation was elevating so higher I started sitting on the same posture for 4 to 6 hours without feeling the sense of time. I became a pure vegetarian since the beginning of the first sadhana, and now it's almost two decades have been passed. Also, I owe to Akashic record for my imagination and bits of knowledge that I cannot explain at any cost. I want to assure you that after completing the exercise for 21 days, you will feel differences; some bad habits will be replaced with auspicious ones, and there will be a change in the point of view of how you see the world. When you complete 45 days, your aura will be more prominent. After practicing it for 108 days you will vibrate in a different energy level and become a magnet of all positivity and possibility. Have faith; you will see the change.

Contents

CHAPTER IV

CHAPTER V

CHAPTER VI

CHAPTER VII

CHAPTER VIII

CHAPTER IX

CHAPTER X

CHAPTER XI

CHAPTER XII

CHAPTER XIII

CHAPTER XIV

CHAPTER XV

CHAPTER I

UNDERSTANDING OF MIND AND BODY

"He who has health, has hope; and he who has hope, has everything."- Thomas Carlyle

It's been ages that humans have always been trying to understand our minds' mysterious and ambiguous nature. The more we get closer to scrutinize it, the more we get lost in the intellectual chaos. Our mind to our body is like software to a robot. The software, for a robot, can neither be seen nor be touched. But the robot is still bounded and limited by the codes and programs. We are more than a robot, yet, very similar to the computers in the context of memory and functioning. The computer's mind is designed with RAM (Random access memory), ROM (Read-only memory), and memory card, so do ours with conscious and sub-conscious. However, the difference is that RAM, ROM, and other memory chips of a computer cannot work together to create a higher level of consciousness, but both levels of mind together can build a whole another state of awareness such as a super-consciousness or cosmic mind. If we use a computer as an analogy to understand our mind, the conscious mind acts as RAM, the sub-conscious mind as ROM, and our brain cells and neurons act as a storage device. As RAM cannot remember anything when the power is cut off, our conscious mind stops working when we are knocked out.

On the other hand, ROM contains the memory where data has been pre-recorded, and its memory is not affected when the power is off. Likewise, the subconscious mind has pre-recorded data of our lives and continues working regardless of the state of our consciousness. I am not trying to compare a computer with the human mind because it is ridiculous. Moreover, it is unfair to compare as computers cannot evolve and our minds, as I mentioned earlier, conscious and subconscious, work together to expand their capability; our minds evolve.

The subconscious mind has pre-recorded data, as I said before, with the help of which our body performs hundreds of activities without our knowledge. We have seen many down-syndrome individuals who are not very connected with our materialistic world and cannot choose a good from the bad. They are not conscious of the environment they are around in many cases. However, their body produces hormones, enzymes, and chemicals. Body temperature, cell division, blood pressure, respiration, digestion, senses, excretion, perspiration, blood clotting, RBC and WBC formation, and thousands of activities are performed immaculately. Conscious mind has no extra-ordinary role or whatsoever in such a case to make life alive. We can analyze entire living organisms, including simpler forms such as cyanobacteria. It is well known that their unicellular body can perform almost as many functions as my trillion-cellular body does. Even microbes can defend themselves against the diseases caused by other phages. A group of scientists from the University of Exeter, United Kingdom, researched if bacteria protect themselves against the virus. On 31st Dec 2017, the research was completed, and they found that bacteria can defend themselves against infection by their immune system called CRISPR-Cas. It seems like the sole purpose of all organisms' life is to live as long as possible. Something is within all of us that is driving us in autopilot mode. This common factor also the autopilot in all organisms is sub-consciousness.

Believe it or not, everything around us is conscious, more or less. Yes, the water, wall, rock, air, and every matter you see and feel is conscious, but some evolve and some not. It all depends on the device of consciousness. By saying device, I mean the body where the consciousness and sub-consciousness stayed. If it is a dog, the level of consciousness is seen higher than water and other inanimate things because a dog, as a device, has more features where conscious and subconscious minds do much more things. For example, If I need to email someone, I can type 70 words per minute on the keyboard. But, if I am given an old version of a cell phone and told to write 50 words of the message, it will take longer. The person who is typing is the same: I still have ten fingers and the same knowledge. However, it will take a long time. It's not because there is a problem with the typist. Actually, the issue is in the device. Similarly, if I am given a device that has only three alphabets, then the job of writing a sensible message will never be done. Likewise, the level of consciousness in everything is similar, but the devices are different from one another. As a result, the output of consciousness can be variant in all animate and inanimate things. In the 1800s, Thomas Young carried out his original double-slit experiment with light, and in 1961, the same experiment was carried out with electrons. In this experiment, there were two screens. One was the entry slit with two openings (holes), say S1 and S2, and the other was there to record where and when an electron hits the detector. When electrons were shot one by one, the detector should record them everywhere on the screen. An individual electron should pass through either S1 or S2. One electron cannot pass through both holes at the same time. Only the wave, say water wave, can pass through both holes simultaneously and create many waves on the other sides that create interference. The outcome was surprising; an electron was behaving like a wave that means it was passing through two holes simultaneously. How is it possible? The experiment was replicated, and the result was the same. Thus, scientists decided to add detectors on each hole to see through which holes the electron was passing and how it could pass through both holes at the same time. Now, the electron was not behaving wave; it was passing through only one hole. When the detector was removed, it acted like a wave, and when detectors were watching it, the electron acted like a particle. Electrons could have interreacted with the detector, scientists thought. Thus, in 1978, physicist John A. proposed a modified version of an experiment called the 'delayed-choice experiment in which two quantum-entangled photons were used at a time. The results indicated that the dual behavior, wave-like or particle-like properties, can also be determined by the decision or plan of the experimenter. In another sense, is the wall not a wall when we don't observe? Everything around us has dual properties, including ourselves, and can be in any form as they like? In 1964, physicist John Bell proposed that when a pair of entangled particles are separated apart in a vast distance, say one on the moon and another on earth, the behavior of one influence the other. If we change the spin of a particle on the earth immediately, the particle's spin on the moon changes. Many experiments have been carried out, and his statement is getting closer to be the truth. How is this twin particle communicating and responding with no time? There is a fundamental force in each particle that science cannot prove to date, but that does not mean it does not exist. The force I am talking about is consciousness. I am reiterating, yes, everything around us is conscious to some extent.

If we look at the great chain of being (a thought by medieval Christianity), a hierarchical structure of all matter, including life, we see the descending rank based on consciousness. It starts from God and ends at all inanimate materials. If we compare the level of consciousness, there should be no place for those who do not have any amount of awareness. The list should get rid of inanimate things if they demonstrate no consciousness at all, and then the comparison is fair among animals, angles, humans, spirit, and God because all of them are conscious. In my opinion, the list is trying to say even though they are inanimate, they have some level of consciousness. It could be undetectable. When an apple is falling from the tree, the earth is moving up towards the apple too. The movement of the earth is so much negligible that nothing can detect it. We know this happens by applying the mathematical formula of gravitation force. Whether it is detectable or not, our interest is not on the level of consciousness of matters. We are just concerned with the truth that cannot be ignored even if it is extremely negligible. According to Upanishads and Sanatan dharma (an ancient Eastern philosophy), everything is conscious. VEDAS (the oldest scriptures) tell us that God exists everywhere and in everything. Vedas see everything in terms of dharma; if the fire is cold, fire has lost its dharma. Dharma basically means the basic characteristics of elements. If this dharma is taken out of an element, the element is dead; there will be no fire without hotness. Thus, that sense of dharma is consciousness, and every single particle of the universe demonstrates its dharma. Puranas (books of history in Sanskrit) tell stories of people communicating with rocks and mountains. In Ramayana (most famous historical event of Bharat & Nepal), when the mother Sita was kidnapped, Ram, the husband of Sita, asked the trees and rocks if they knew about her.

Coming back to the point, we were discussing conscious and sub-conscious minds. The conscious mind is curios, argumentative, cunning, and quarrelsome. The conscious mind as the gatekeeper does not allow any belief system to pass through it to reach the sub-conscious level. Whereas the subconscious mind is very straightforward, hardworking, honest, and believer. The subconscious mind is the one that keeps us alive as well as turns our thoughts into reality, but it does not have any direct contact with our physical world. If our thoughts manage to fool our conscious mind and slip through the gate, the subconscious mind accepts it as pre-recorded codes and works on it to make it a reality. It does not understand right and wrong. Bhagavad Geeta (a must-read book), in chapter 6, verse number 6, says, "For those who have conquered the mind, it is their friend. For those who have failed to do so, the mind works as an enemy." The way to reach our inner consciousness is through the conscious mind, and we must learn to tame it.

When we are kids, the level of the conscious mind is low, but the activities of the sub-conscious mind are high. The subconscious mind continuously records anything that happens around us; it never rests. At this early age, a child has less reasoning power. Thus, the conscious mind is not tough enough to block the information from reaching the subconscious mind. Not all information he comes across pass through the gate of the conscious mind. However, a few of them indeed do, and that accepted information shapes the child's future. This is why we should not say any negative words in front of kids or anyone. Before we turn 15, we are associated with thousands of negative sentences such as 'you can't do this, 'you are dumb,' 'you are a loser,' and so on. A few of those make it to the subconscious level and work in making us dumb. We do not know how many negative thoughts were planted into our subconscious mind when we were a child. As a result, most of us are depressed, unhappy, and a failure today. Many types of research have been done, and the results have demonstrated the tremendous power of the subconscious mind.

Now, it is time to clear all negativities that we have accumulated in our subconscious minds. The first step here is to become a friend with the conscious mind. Without taming it, we achieve nothing. The conscious mind feeds information through our senses and is very mischievous and restless like a monkey. We need to attract the attention of this wild monkey. There are some effective techniques I am going to discuss below regarding the taming and purification of the mind.

Auto-Suggestion

i) A research paper published on 8th of October, 2017, 'The role of autosuggestion in geriatric patients' quality of life' concluded that the autosuggestion is significantly associated with improvement of geriatrics' quality of life, including serum cortisol level as well as adaptive immunity (Sari and et al., 2017). The most beautiful explanation with examples can be found in Psycho-Cybernetics, written by Dr. Maxwell Maltz in 1960. Dr. Maltz was a plastic/cosmetic surgeon whose job was to fix the distorted parts in the body or face and make people beautiful again. He found most of his clients sad even after the stunning transformation. He realized the main reason behind their sadness, and named it 'self-image.' No matter what others think about you, the thing that matters is what you feel about yourself. That was the self-image idea. Buddha also said, "We are what we think. All that we are arise with our thoughts. With our thoughts, we construct the world." If we have a negative self-image, then how to replace it with the auspicious one? Dr. Maltz realized that autosuggestion could bring the change. He told his clients to stand in front of the mirror and speak nicely about themselves every morning for at least 21 days. He saw positive changes in his clients.

Autosuggestion really boosts the confidence of an individual. Now, coming to the point: how to use autosuggestion to replace our negativity in the subconscious mind? Write down and make a list of things that you want in your life. When you have a list, choose the most vital one. Make the number of sentences from 5 to 10. Now, edit the sentences. Tried to use as few words as possible to complete the wish. For example, I am happy. Be specific, not vague. Complete the sentence and do not use negative words such as not, never, ever, etc. Instead of saying I am never poor, say I am a millionaire. Make a compelling list of your wish.

ii) **Get a rosary bead, sit on any meditation posture and start chanting the list of affirmations that you created.** You will have to chant 21 times in the morning and 21 times right before bed for 21 days. If you cannot accomplish this, you won't be able to achieve anything in upcoming chapters. If you are one of my students and reading this book, you know the deal; until you pass through the 21 days of purification phase, the teaching does not get any further. If you are reading this by will, you want to progress in materialistic and spiritual life. Thus, I trust you on this, and I hope you will do what I recommend in every chapter in this book.

Deep Breathing Practice (Yogic Breathing)

According to a research paper published in 2002 by Dr. Saaresranta and Dr. Polo, 'Hormones and Breathing,' several hormones such as testosterone, progesterone, growth hormones, and so on are involved in the control of breathing. Hormones are directly related to breathing. So, if we control our breathing consciously, there will be some changes in the production and effect of those hormones. Scientists have found that deep breathing calms down an angry individual's temper and solves many other health issues. On the other hand, this will provide plenty of oxygen to the cell. When the cell gets enough oxygen, they perform their job effectively and effortlessly; the load on the subconscious mind is decreased. When the subconscious mind has less load, the conscious mind feels like it did its job flawlessly. In this moment of pride, our mind acts as our friend. Deep breathing has a significant impact on our saliva and enzyme production as well. A study done by Dr. Sundar Balasubramanian and his team at the Medical University of South Carolina in 2016 discovered that the individuals practicing deep breathing exercises produce more salivary nerve growth factors (NFG), which can be important for treating Alzheimer's disease. Also, they discovered that this breathing practice stimulates the protein that suppresses tumors and builds up our immune responses(immunoglobulins).

Breathing through each nostril has a different meaning in yoga and its effects on the mind and body. I am going to touch a small part of Tantra (technique or practice) here. When I was learning Mantra-Tantra-Yantra under the supervision of my Guru, it took me seven months to win the trust and confidence of my Guru to prove that I master my breathing and I am worthy enough for further training. It's not the student who should claim his worthiness; when a student is ready, Guru himself shows him the way. One day my Guru observed me practicing pranayama secretly from far, and after two hours, when I was done, he came to me and said, "Be here before sunrise tomorrow; you are practicing control over kundalini shakti." I was glad that finally, I moved forward in the spiritual journey. I will discuss a bit of the technique I was taught in Tantra about breathing. For this, we need to know Nadis. Nadis are tunnels in our body through which the life force, prana, circulates. Shiva Samhita, a highly revered tantric book, says there are 14 main Nadis. Ida, Pingala, and Sushumna are the essential ones for our mental and physical health. I am just putting them here for your knowledge. You are still not ready for pranayama.

i) **Ida:** Your left nostrils are considered to be Ida which is related to the moon. The tunnel originates from the base chakra, Muladhara, and ends up in the left nostril. You can check your breathing; if the air is circulating freely through the left nostril, then ida is dominant. Since this ida is associated with the moon, it cools down your body and makes you imaginative. You can make a proper decision on anything when the prana is circulating through this nostril. If your daily life is stressful where you have to make many decisions, it is suggested that you should sleep on the right side, which opens the left nostril. In researches, it is found that sleeping on the right side helps in insomnia and snoring.

ii) **Pingla:** This is associated with the sun and is the right nostril. It also originates from Muladhara and ends up in the right nostril. As it is related to the sun, it generates heat and energy in the channel of our system. All labor workers or physical trainers are suggested to sleep on the left side. Especially a heavy meal(dinner), we must rest on the left so that the Sun Nadi gets activated, digests the food effectively in a short time, and provide a maximum amount of energy.

iii) **Sushumna:** This is the central channel or tunnel which connects Muladhara to Sahasrara (crown chakra). We can say, the central part inside the spine is its physical location. Until we clean up this canal through which prana flows, the optimum amount of upward movement of energy through each kundalini cannot happen.

Every day, I hear and read people practicing kundalini activation methods. There are a lot of self-proclaimed gurus on YouTube promising success in this field. You should not worry about it right now. Just focus on deep breathing; be mindful about it. Try to inhale as much oxygen as you can through both nostrils, expanding stomach, and exhale all air through the mouth by contracting the abdomen and chest. You do not need to worry about holding it for now. Just breathe in and out, but the deep one without any difficulty.

Visualization

This is a very compelling idea while talking about fooling the conscious mind. The conscious mind is not gullible; it requires solid proofs to make it believe anything. For example, if I say I am a millionaire while my bank balance is $200. No matter how many times I repeat this mantra, the conscious mind rejects it, and my wish never reaches the sub-conscious mind. Something or someone can be so stubborn and decisive. However, everything and everyone has some weaknesses. The greatest weakness of the conscious mind is that it relies on our senses to accumulate information and depends on our emotions to examine if it is correct. It follows the motto, "seeing is believing." Yet, it scrutinizes the info on several levels. If it was that easy, like saying 'seeing is believing, everything we dream while sleeping would come true. Before discussing techniques, we need to know the reality that the conscious mind understands. Scientifically speaking, everything we see as reality is the virtual impression of things around us. Light goes into our brain and creates the image exactly in the same manner that we imagine a picture in our mind. In both scenarios, no solid matter goes into our minds. For example, if my friend is standing next to his life-size photo or wax-statue, my brain will process both images. If those images were put in front of the subconscious mind, it would take both as accurate, but the conscious mind immediately distinguishes fake from the real. This is because reality is not only associated with seeing but also with feelings. Following techniques add the effectiveness on visualization method:

1. **Feeling or emotions:** It is imperative to relate feelings and emotions with any information to fool the conscious mind. Let's take an example of a movie. You know that is not real life, but still, you cry when your favorite character is in agony. When you are feeding information to the conscious mind, you overload it with emotions that compel the conscious mind in believing the information provided is true (someone close is in pain) and communicates with the subconscious mind to produce hormones such as estrogen and cortisol. As a result, you cry. You really do not have to see an image either. You can just imagine a picture of your loved one and put some emotions to it; tears will be in your eyes. Don't you cry when you miss your mother because, now, she will never come back to you?

2. **Repetition:** Nothing can really beat the hard work of persistence. When someone is persistent in achieving something, sooner or later, the person meets his goal. A woodcutter successfully chops down a massive tree by hitting it repeatedly. Even the water droplets can poke a hole on rocks when it hits on the same spot continuously. It is said that if you stick around the barbershop for long enough, sooner or later, you get the haircut. Do the visualization practice repeatedly with full emotions; your conscious mind will have nothing left besides passing your bill to the sub-conscious mind.

Vibration

There is no doubt that we all are made up of vibration. When an electron absorbs a photon, it jumps to the higher energy level, to the next shell. That higher level is temporary. To maintain that energy level for the electron, a continuous supply of photons is a must. As soon as the supply is cut off, it loses the energy and falls back to the same old shell. Similarly, when a person suddenly changes his vibration by mimicking others or in the influence of others, he is not a permanent guess of that energy level. Indeed, he falls back onto his previous status. If you want to change your life, change the vibration of your mind and body. It is easy to analyze people in terms of vibration when we see them. The vibration of success, happiness, and wellness is more challenging to attain than sadness, failure, and uneasiness. I met a person who told me that she never met or saw a particular class/race of prosperous, honest, and helpful people. I disagreed because most of the people I know from that specific group are the opposite of what she told me. Later on, I contemplated over it. Then, I concluded that you see the world based on what frequency you are vibrating. A thousand dollars means a lot for some people, but for Bezos, the richest man in the world, losing or gaining a thousand does not make a difference in his wealthiness. The woman I talked to was a college dropout, working in Wal-Mart with minimum wage, no personal achievements, and no professional success. When you vibrate in this low frequency, you won't attract others vibrating at a higher energy level. Even if you do, it will not go well. If you want to be in Paris, you must go to Paris. By visiting every place in Japan, it is stupidity to conclude that there is no Eiffel Tower in the world. I have tried to put all brain waves in the following chart to see how they look different.

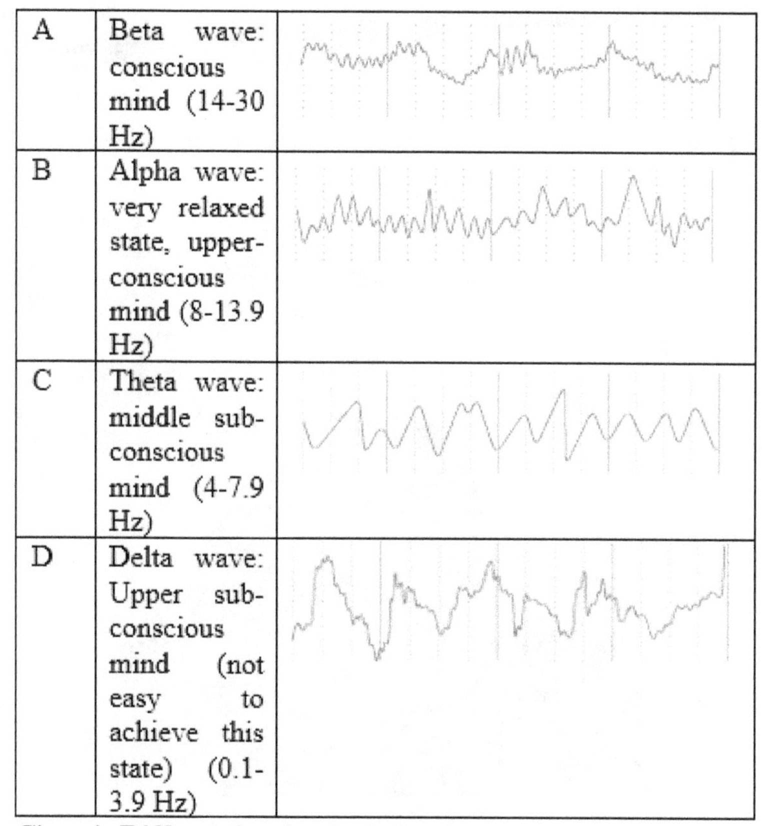

A	Beta wave: conscious mind (14-30 Hz)	
B	Alpha wave: very relaxed state, upper-conscious mind (8-13.9 Hz)	
C	Theta wave: middle sub-conscious mind (4-7.9 Hz)	
D	Delta wave: Upper sub-conscious mind (not easy to achieve this state) (0.1-3.9 Hz)	

Chart.1: Different levels of mind and their respective waves.

When we analyze the chart above, we see that the frequency of the conscious mind is higher than any other level. In this state, our mind is vigilant and restless. All the negativities such as anxiety, conflict, depression, agitation, worry, and energy lessness exist in this phase. As the mind evolves and moves upward towards higher consciousness, the reasoning power goes down, alertness vanishes, and conflict does not exist. As a result, at the best level that it can be, the frequency will be shallow. What happens when the frequency is zero? That simply means the person is dead. There is no way that the living brain emits zero Hz frequency. Even when one is in a deeper state of samadhi, his brain will continue to release the wave.

Let's analyze the above graphs in a different approach. When a person is in the conscious state of mind, he has hundreds of thoughts producing a higher wave frequency. That means more energy is exiting his mind, on the conscious level, leaving him behind vibrating in a low energy zone. When someone continuingly loses power, his mind does not potentially attract vibrating things at higher energy levels. In the following chart, I tried to classify the energy levels of people we see around us.

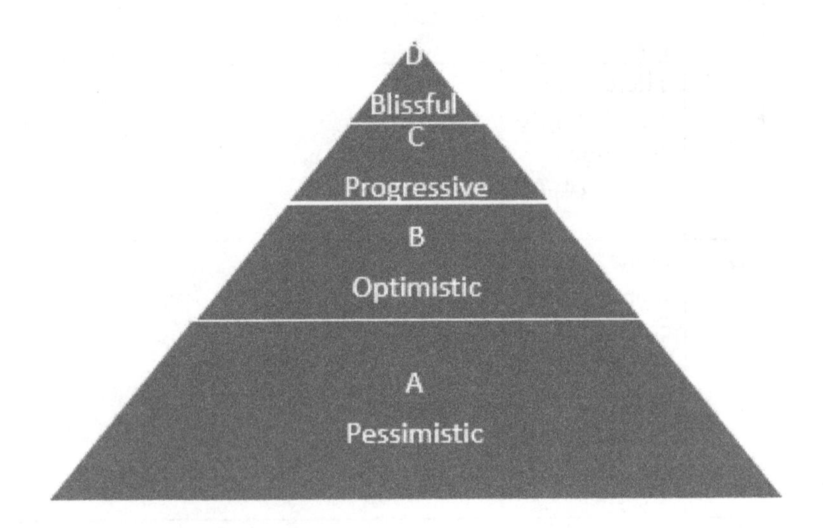

This is just a general picture I tried to show you here about the energy level of different types of people. On the bottom level, people who are in conscious level all the time fall in. Primarily, this group of people only see a negative aspect first. If you give them a blank paper with a small stain on it, they will argue about that small area with a stain. I want to tell you a story about the nature of this type of people, the story I heard a long time ago from my teacher.

A long time ago, there was a king whose kingdom was wealthy, and he was doing pretty good in ruling the country. One day, he decided to visit the countryside with his prime Minister in disguise to investigate the progress of his regime. They traveled all day, and the King was satisfied with the prosperity of his kingdom. In the evening, while returning palace, just a few miles away from the palace, he saw a shabby old hut. King imagined the hardship of the family living there and felt sorry for them. He decided to investigate the situation. Thus, both of them walked towards the hut. When they reached the courtyard of the house, they heard the laughter of kids and woman. King took a peek through the window and saw the farmer and his family having a good time. The King was baffled.

"How can anybody be this happy in such an adversity?" He asked the prime Minister. The King seemed stressed because he was the King, yet he did not have time to play with the prince and always had some issues to resolve. As a result, he was never happy. Seeing the King sad, the Prime Minister said, "Dear king, this family is in bliss because they are not busy counting coins."

"What does the counting coins mean?" King asked in confusion.

"Give me a bag of 99 gold coins, I will tell you, actually show you what I mean."

King was curious to know what the Prime Minister was planning to do. He agreed to give him 99 gold coins. After six months, King and the Prime Minister decided to visit the same family to see the result. When they reached the hut, King did not hear any laughter. Instead, the man was arguing with his wife. The King was surprised to see the difference.

"What happened to the happiness they had?" the King asked.

"Counting coin took it," Minister replied. He further explained, "I put the bag of 99 coins on his doorstep. After seeing the bag, he started counting the coins. There were 99 of them. He could not believe such an odd figure and counted over and over, hoping for 100.

He asked his wife to recount to make sure the number, but the number was still the same. He started thinking about the missing one. He lost his sleep thinking about the ways to make one more coin so that he would have a full 100. He started working hard to earn one more coin. He spent 6 months but could not make it. One day, his wife took five coins for shopping. Seeing five coins missing, the farmer got mad, and the peace of household was disappeared. In summary, the day after I put coins on his doorstep, he and his family lost the happiness."

"But the gold was supposed to make him happier," King asked.

"Yes, but many people don't enjoy what they have. They are worried about what is missing. This farmer was happy when he did not have any coins, but when he found some, he got busy in counting and worrying for nonexistent ones."

Likewise, a lot of people around us care about the things they don't have and eventually lose what they have too. If we have a close look at the pyramid above, we see the area A, B, C, and D that is the same notation I used for the brain chart. So, I am talking about the same phenomenon but differently. In the figure, we notice that the area of room A is the largest one. I named it pessimistic, but it refers to many more. All negativities such as greed, violence, hatred, and selfishness fall in this category. Also, those who accept defeat easily have the vibration related to this area. The most significant part of today's human population occupies this room. If somebody lived his entire life in this room, nobody could make him understand the elements that can be experienced in B, C, or D zone. Everyone he meets, everything he sees, and everything he receives has precisely the same energy level. People do not understand that they are attracting those, and they blame others or the situations that are not pleasant to them. There is no other way than jumping into another energy pool to change the cycle of attracting and receiving low-energy stuff.

Optimistic level, room B, is far better than room A. The person who has control over his unnecessary thoughts and wills falls into this category. His level of decision-making is higher. As you go up in the pyramid, the delta level is the blissful one which is almost impossible for most people to attain. There is one quick way to increase our inner energy level and control the overflow of high-frequency waves out of mind. It is the vibration of kindness that alleviates the state of mind. To test this hypothesis, you can conduct an experiment. Go and buy a beautiful watch that you want to wear. Instead of keeping it for yourself, gift it to your friend or relative. Every time you meet him, how do you feel to see him wearing that watch?

Research has shown that people get more happiness when they spend money on others than on themselves. If you want to expedite enhancing the inner energy level, you should secretly donate to the poor. You should neither make a video of you donating nor take any pictures for posing later. If you are donating money, knowledge, labor, or anything worthwhile, you are already different from a vast number of people. Don't degrade your vibration by flexing it on social media. Every action has a reaction. Don't compromise your divine activities for such a mediocre reaction; you are worth better than that, and since the action has been done, the universe will indeed offer you the best response you deserve. Many people may disagree and say that if you make a video of you donating, many people will learn from you, and everyone starts helping each other. First of all, helping someone for the name and fame won't motivate anyone for long. Instead, people start making fake videos of such acts and will create too many evils. On the other hand, our goal is not to teach anyone about anything at this point in time. We are just trying to enhance our inner energy level. There is no other way than to help others in need secretly to jump into a higher mental state; this is my personal experience. Especially when you see the person's happiness, and you know that you are the reason, what else can make you so satisfied than this? I will discuss this aspect more in later Chapter VII; The Wealth.

There are so many more minor things that can make us mentally and emotionally strong such as the feeling of gratitude, forgiving people to the level they deserve (Why not to forgive everyone, I have discussed it in detail in chapterVIII, The Courage), and accepting everything as it is. Most of the time, we take many things for granted, like we are entitled to them, but not. Remember, we get what we deserve, not what we want. The way to make ourselves well-deserving is to switch our inner vibration and get ourselves into the upper level, as shown in the pyramid.

Another method to change our vibration is listening to the sound of the singing bowl, the real kind, not the recorded one. Research published in 2020 by Jessica Stanhope and Phillip Weinstein on 'the human health effects of singing bowls' suggests that the benefit of the singing bowl may get more effective when the patients themselves create the vibration. Also, if the bowl touches the specific part of the patient's body, the beat would work more effectively (Stanhope et al., 2020) because it is all about the vibration but not the sound. Those who enjoy guided meditation and binaural sound may find this painful. I disagree with the research on the point that recorded sound does not give any vibration. The effect is undoubtedly less, but recorded sound can also give us goosebumps and allows us to vibrate at different energy levels. However, I do not suggest listening to random sounds on YouTube. Until you produce vibration by yourself, you won't realize what I am talking about. Coming back to the singing bowl, though some patients felt better while doing the bowl therapy, the physical comforts did not last long; as soon as the treatment was over, the pain reappeared. However, the research did not find any adverse effect.

As I already mentioned, staying at a better vibration level for a long time with the help of external efforts is not possible. The vibration of every single cell may respond and mimic the vibration they are surrounded with, but as soon as the energy is gone, the electron shall fall back to the previous energy level. If you follow each step mentioned in this book, you don't have to worry about falling back into the old energy pool. It is easy to fall down than to jump up.

The best way to increase the inner energy level is by chanting 'OM.' It took me more than 1 year to create a decent sound. Not even the so-called many meditation gurus I have seen can produce this sound with the right note. I am not talking about the quality of voice or sound either; I am talking about the phenomenon of hitting the exact spots(chakras) in the body and creating a resonance of the sound for exact amount of time. It is surprising for you to know that we can make the effect of vibration (not the vibration) just by chanting it in your mind. That's the possibility. To achieve this, you need to do 'Mantra Sadhana' under the supervision of a Siddha Guru.

I do not suggest you start chanting 'OM' right away because you are in the beginning phase of purification. By the end of this book, when you practice all the book's easy steps and analyze your results, you will see where you stand. Don't worry about the teacher; a teacher will appear when the student is ready. Anyway, you do not need to sweat about the chanting for the success of materialistic life.

Since everything is made up of vibration, we can cure diseases by killing pathogens using vibration without clinical surgery. In 1934, Royal Rife did a detailed study about viruses and proposed a theory that all organisms resonate at their own specific frequency, accepted in quantum physics. Those pathogens do good in the host body when the frequency of the host cell is lowered. This means, if we succeed in raising our inner energy level, the pathogen cannot overcome the effect of our vibration, and eventually, our higher frequency explodes their cell membrane and kill them.

Habit Of Writing Journal

Writing is critical when we talk about reaching the subconscious level. I am not saying typing; you must write on paper in ink with your hand. Most of the successful people throughout history have kept journals. Writing a journal helps us track our health and success. It sharpens our memory. It also makes us more disciplined. I write two types of journals daily, and I have found them very auspicious in all aspects of my life.

Dream Tracking Notebook

I track my dreams to know the state of my subconscious mind. Most of the time, I find the answer that I ask before bed. If I do not write it as soon as I get up, I will not have detailed information. Most possibly, I may forget the details entirely. I usually keep a pen and a notebook next to my bed. I write the details of the dream even if I wake up middle of the night. You cannot ignore them and fall asleep if you want to get what you desire. You must strive hard for success as much as you do for a breath while drowning.

Day-To-Day Journal

This general journal has proven to be a phenomenal method to record your emotions and daily happening. This not only strengthens your memory but also shows you a lucid vision of your life. On the other hand, just following these successful daily life hacks, you will find yourself vibrating in different levels, and for the proof, you can see the change in your journal records every week or month. Only the problem is to start and persist the activities. You will start, there is no doubt, but will give up soon too. Don't give up on yourself.

There is another type of journal that I have been writing since 2015 and I have found it extremely helpful for my economic growth. I will discuss about it later in chapter VII; The Wealth.

There could be a lot of other methods to purify the mind (we are not touching any aspects meditation and 8 limbs of yoga here), but these above five techniques are strictly required to adhere for my students to learn further because I have been through these and know their effects.

We talked about the purification of the mind; now, it's time to purify our body as well. A healthy mind living in a miserable body is not more than filling the tank of a wheel-less car with super unleaded gas. Health is wealth. For success in any field, physical fitness plays a vital role. There are infinite ways to maintain fitness and purify our bodies. I will discuss only those that I have been doing for years.

Our body produces a lot of toxins while sleeping. Also, we need to dilute the digestive acid that our stomach produces all night. The following methods have helped me stay healthy.

a. **Starting the day with a few sips of water in a pure copper cup:** When you go to bed at night, fill the cup with water. Make sure that you use a copper cup only; avoid the plastic ones. If you do not have a copper cup, use a glass one for today. But you need to buy it as soon as possible and make sure it is 100% copper. Copper has consistently been recognized for its antimicrobial properties for thousands of years. On February 1st, 2019, research was published on 'Antibacterial efficacy of wire arc sprayed copper coatings against various pathogens' by Arda Kocaman and Ozgul Keles. "The spray gun was used to spray the copper onto stainless steel. The coating morphology was examined by scanning electron microscope and its structure determined by x-ray diffraction (Kocaman et al., 2019)." After the experiment, all the bacteria types were effectively eliminated. The result shows that the copper coating has a strong killing effect on the pathogen. It can kill viruses and other germs by disrupting the protective layers of the cell of the organisms. The atomic structure, chemical foundation, and vibration of the copper are intolerable for simpler cell organisms. Thus, the copper cup can act as a natural filter for your water. However, do not try drinking dirty water on the copper cup. I noticed that some people get side effects on digestion after drinking water in a copper cup, and they have diarrhea. This could be because your cup is not 100% pure copper, and you swallowed some copper coating. This can cause the level of copper intake high in your body. Too much copper can damage the good bacteria that live in the intestine. As a result, you will have diarrhea. Continue drinking for a week and see if you have the same issue. I hope your body will get used to it, and you will be able to continue drinking in a copper cup.

As soon as you get up, take a few sips of water, don't chug it. This has to be done before you go to the bathroom for urination. After that, you can write the dream tracking journal and go for a daily routine. The water you drank not only dilutes the acid in your stomach but also hydrates you. You do not want to chug the cup of water.

b. A special recipe for boiled water: In 2015, I got the flu and became sick for almost two weeks. The cold turned into the sinus. Medicine was not helping me. Then, I decided to research Ayurveda, an ancient way of healing, and come up with my recipe. The suggested combination was complex. Some of the herbs were rare. So, I decided to make my own recipe with household herbs which are available in every kitchen. I have never been ill after that to date.

Things required:

1. Water
2. Ginger
3. Turmeric
4. Honey
5. Lemon
6. Cloves
7. Cardamom
8. Cinnamon sticks

Boil the mixture and drink while it is hot. I have found it very helpful in cold, diarrhea, dizziness, and so on. You can add other kinds of stuff as you want, but for the benefit we want, this is more than capable for our purpose. If you wish to have more energy, add honey. Otherwise, the chances of gaining weight are high for less active people. If you do not have all ingredients, you should have water, ginger, and lemon for positive effects. You need to drink this mixture at least 20-30 min before breakfast. If you do so, it cleanses your blood and helps in thinning it, which eventually helps in reducing the heart attack, boosts immune, strengthens digestion, lowers cholesterol, acts as anti-inflammation, and does much more. However, do not put much of turmeric and ginger because they can affect you adversely too. Too much ginger can cause an upset stomach. I did not mention the quantity of the ingredient you should mix because I never measured it before making it. Just go with your taste.

Fasting

This is the most effective method, I must say, based on my experiences. In many cultures, all around the world, people fast for various purposes. In my family, fasting is a very essential element of happiness. I will not explain why I love fasting because I don't want to give you a hypothetical explanation. In this book, I stick with the scientific research and proofs only to back up my perspective so that you can trust me and my words.

According to a research paper published on 13th May 2020, 'Unravelling the health effects of fasting' by Francoise Wilhelmi de Toledo and the team, fasting was extra-ordinarily helpful for a healthy life. Key- messages of the research paper are as follows:

1. "Biochemical changes during fasting are characterized by a glucose to ketone switch, leading to a rise of ketones, advantageously used for brain energy, with consequent improved cognition."

2. "Ketones reduce appetite and help maintain effective fasting."

3. "Application of fasting patterns increases healthy life span and defenses against oxidative and metabolic stresses." (Toledo and et al., 2020)

You can pick a day when you are not physically active and try not to eat for 24 hours but can drink as much water as you want. Every time you feel hungry, you must drink water to dilute the gastric acid and hydrochloric acid. People drink juice, but I don't. If you need some energy, drink the water, as I said, with honey and a minimum amount of ginger and turmeric. When I am fasting, I do as follow:

1. Drink plenty of plain water and a few cups of the mixture you prepared earlier.
2. Stay outside for enough sunbathing and sweating as much as possible.
3. No caffeine and soda at all.
4. Nicotine, tobacco, or alcohol is strictly prohibited.
5. Routine physical exercise like walking should be done.

Pick a day for greens only: You must do this task once a week to purify your body. You have to go without meat, egg, dairy, fish, and other animal products. Honey is fine. This is the hardest part of the diet that people cannot follow. They cannot eat vegetables for one day. I am not saying that you should eat more meat the next day. If you can stay away from animal products consuming as food, beneficial for you, but I don't force you to go vegetarian. I quit eating meat when I was a kid, and now it's been 20 years. Green vegetables are healthy food, and it does not need a research paper to prove it; we all know about it.

Colon Cleansing

The gut must be healthy because it is considered as the second brain. There are a few effective methods to clean the colon. I have discussed the ones I have tried on myself and found worthwhile. They are:

1. **Yogic colon cleansing method (Laghu Sankhaprakshalana Kriya)**
   This practice is associated with some yoga asanas. If I have to cleanse my colon, I chug 3 cups of Luke-warm salted water. This time sipping does not work. You have to chug as fast as you can. You will have to learn some asanas from somebody, or google will help you to find pictures if you type the name of

Kriya as I wrote inside the bracket above. This is a very effective technique; all yogis follow this cleansing method. According to research on 'Effect of yogic colon cleansing on health' done on Jan 1st, 2019, this yogic practice can be suggested in bowl treatment regularly. It does not have any side effects and can be done once a week for a month (Kiran and et al., 2019). I won't suggest doing it every day or every week throughout the year.

2. **Enemas:** This method is effective but can only be carried out in privacy. I personally perform this four times a year. My approach is more complicated than the typical one. I fast for at least two to three days before I carry out this method. Every time I cleanse my colon, I feel healthy, energetic, and rejuvenated. A few different techniques work for me, but I do not want to put them here because I do not know if it works for others. I do not want to give a random suggestion that might have worked only for me.

Caring For Bio-Diversity Within Us

It is needless to say that the number of bacteria or microorganisms living on and in our body outnumber human cells by 10 to 1. This means 10 microorganisms per human cell. This signifies that our existence depends upon their activities. Every single human is different biodiversity of these microorganisms. While we are taking care of our own cells, we need to take care of these little friends. An article published on September 1st, 2019, 'Can microbes boost your mood?' by Caitlin Dow, shows that these microbes could play a role in mental health. They produce the byproduct that dissolves in the blood, and the brain releases the hormones based on the information it received from microbes. They influence our mood and try to work to better our health because we are theirs home. Actually, we both are co-existing. Thus, we need to recognize them. To take care of this microbes, we should do as follows:

1. **Food:** We need to eat the food they like to produce good chemicals and protect their own bio-diversity. If we don't focus on maintaining their population and health, other harmful microbes will take over the bio-diversity and kill them. This will result in making us weak, sick, and unhealthy. We need to know our friendly microbes and feed them well. The foods that help them flourished are such as beans, lentils, peas, broccoli, whole grains, raspberries, fruits, and greens.

2. **Medicines kill them:** When we take medicine for anything, we get addicted to drugs. We must avoid taking medication as much as possible. These are not only harmful to our cells but also vigorously detrimental to the good microbes. When 90% of our body (by number) is unhealthy and dying, our 10% (by number) of cells will not be able to fight against harmful microbes. As a result, we will suffer from various diseases. I have not encountered any drug without its side effects. No matter how much a doctor advocates about the effectiveness of drugs, I highly doubt it, especially the side effects. If you must take medicines to stay alive, go for it, but just for head ache, stomach ache, and minor pain, do not reach out to take medication. Listen to your body and slowly find out what your gut wants, what your microbes desire, and what is ultimately good for you.

With these words, I have shown you the most effective way to cleanse your gut and to take care of the bio-diversity of microbes living within us that work day and night to make us healthy and happy.

Summary Of Chapter I

Everything I told you to do, I did it. I am still doing it. Thus, there should be no doubts about these exercises and their effectiveness. If you are not motivated enough for your own success, then who would? This chapter aims to make you healthy from the inside out and cancel all negativities you have in your subconscious mind. Be determined and optimistic to start another chapter. I am positive about your efforts, and there is no doubt that you will reach your destination at the end of this book, but the minimum period is two and half months to shed the old you and regenerate an animated version of you.

1. **Wake-up time: 6 A.M.**
2. **Drink water, sip by sip.**
3. **Write dream tracking journal.**
4. **Drink the boiled water with my recipe.**
5. **Practice breathing in an open area.**
6. **Chant the mantra you created.**
7. **Practice visualization (does not have to be in the morning).**
8. **Be kind all day.**
9. **Eat healthy.**
10. **Chant the mantra you created before bed.**

CHAPTER II

STRENGTH

"When the time comes, you need to be able to win without fighting."

I made the title vague intentionally. I could have been more specific, writing it as physical strength, mental strength, or so on, but I did not do so for a few reasons. If I say physical strength, I will miss the opportunity to discuss other important aspects of life. In this chapter, I will discuss some areas of life and physical body to strengthen. I will mention only those that I found extra-ordinarily auspicious for my materialistic and spiritual world.

Physical Strength

Being healthy is different from being strong. You may have 25% body fat and still be healthy, but when we talk about being strong, we are talking about the volume and the quality of the muscles. If you have more fat and less muscle, then muscles won't perform their function effectively; they cannot bear the load of your own weight. As a result, you have back pain, knee pain, and so on. When we see a big guy, we think he must be powerful, but not really. The functions of muscles and fat are vastly different. Muscle involves locomotion by connection to the bone, maintaining the posture of the body. It is made up of muscle fibers. Whereas fat involves storing lipids and substances in the fat cell and using them as energy when required. According to the result finding of the research, 'Effects of muscle strengthening around the hip on pain, physical function, and gait in elderly patients' by KwangSun do and JongEun Yim on Nov 17th, 2020, a 12- week muscle strengthening exercise program improved the pain, physical function, and gait patterns of patients (Yim and et al., 2020). In any posture, if you will to meditate and have a weak back, you won't be able to sit for long. If your hamstring, quadriceps, and calf muscles are ailing, the knee movements will be impeded, and your health will be impaired. You must focus on building more muscles and lowering fat as much as possible. By saying it, I don't mean you have to join a gym and start bodybuilding. However, I strongly suggest you focus on strengthening your entire muscles, including the core. I keep on changing my body weight. My cycle of gaining and losing weight lasts 6 months. When I hit 190 pounds and above, fat below 16%, I switch on losing programs to cut fat percentage to make in between 8%-12%. I prefer to have a nice toned muscle than the bulgy one with a high percentage of fat. Since I am a pure vegetarian, losing weight is super easy, and the opposite is tough. I don't sweat about the result anyway; I just focus on my hard work. I do weight training most. When I am traveling, I pick some indoor exercises. Bodyweight exercises that worked very well for me are as follows:

1. **Muscle failure:** I learned the concepts and effects of these exercises when I was a soldier. Researches have proved that reaching muscle failure while lifting or resisting weights or exceeding the point with one more set result in the growth of more muscles. If you do 70 push-ups in two minutes and reach muscle failure but continue 2-5 more repetitions, you will gain more muscles. Do all sorts of exercises to strengthen your hamstrings, biceps, back, chest, triceps, shoulders, calves, and all muscles of your body.

2. **A long walk or short sprint:** personally, I really don't like to run for long. If I do, 3-5 miles is the maximum, and the speed

would be 6-8 mph on average. However, I do sprint several times to increase my heartbeat to inhale and consume oxygen. While running, sprinting, walking, or exercising, do not forget to have deep breathing as many as you can. When I am on the trimming phase (the phase when I lose weight), I run 6 times a week for 30 minutes each day. I sprint only 3 times a week and less than 20 min each trial in the gaining phase. Walking has some extraordinary benefits that I have experienced personally in my life. When I am walking, I am self-talking in my mind. Many future plans I made or many desires I had in the past have come true. There is a link between creativity and movement of legs, I mean walking. According to a study published in standford news on apr 24th, 2014, standford researchers found that walking boosts a person's creative output by an average of 60%. Thus, start walking alone, be mindful about breathing and think about the wishes you like to see in the future. Never be negative. Even if there are real problems and issues you face, always think positive and hope for the best. I am sure, sooner or later, you will find the solution to each problem.

3. **Puzzle and logical games:** you may think this category had to be under mental strength. Actually not. When we play logical games and puzzles, they help strengthen our brain by affecting grey matter, which is a part of the physical body. While solving puzzles, our brain's hunting character comes out. It tries to find the answer. When we figure out the last clue, a rush of dopamine flows into our bloodstream, and we feel good. There is no solid proof on puzzles and games strengthening memory. A research paper published in 1999 found no evidence to suggest that puzzles and games reduce age-related decline in cognition. Still, we want to train our brain in the logical aspects of decision making and the regular creation and release of the happy hormone dopamine.

4. **Playing chess:** if you do not know the game, learn it. You cannot exclude this from your daily routine. I have been playing chess daily for years. I don't play to win or brag about it, and I am not the best at playing either. I play 2-3 games a day. You can download the game on your phone that allows you to compete with a real person all over the world. Chess not only teaches you discipline but also makes you intuitive. You will learn deep thinking. When you play chess enough, you will imagine many consecutive consequences that may follow one after another before it happens. Chess allows you to learn a lesson that every moves you make in the present has an inevitable impact on the future. Chess also teaches you to be persistent on your goals. I have personally felt that chess can take you to a different energy level. It slows down your thought process and enhances your concentration level. A research journal was published on dec 19th, 2019, by juan pedro fuentes-garcia and the team on 'chess players increase the theta power spectrum when the difficulty of the opponent increase.' participants who won games when the difficulty level was increased, their brain wave showed the increment in the theta wave, and those who lost the game showed even higher theta power (garcia and et al., 2019). If you pause and think about the waves, you realize the beauty of this game. Brain releases theta wave when the deep subconscious mind takes charge. This is very pleasant to know that you will access the subconscious mind whether you win or lose the game. Another research paper published on July 24th, 2014, by adrain m. Siegel and team on 'the architecture of the chess player's brain' concluded that there will be some morphological changes in the brain of chess players as they activate different brain areas while they are engaged in chess-related activities (siegel and et al., 2014). Thus, chess proved to be a mental exercise that allows us to fool the conscious mind, and now, don't you want to play chess?

Verbal Strength

No, neither am I talking about memorizing thousands of unheard words like in SAT or GRE nor telling you to be extra fluent in the language. My intention is pointing towards the communication skill while I am saying verbal strength. You need to work on the effectiveness of your communication skill if you don't have them. A language is not knowledge, but it is a power that can help you to achieve greatness with less or no effort. Honestly speaking, English is my fourth language, and thus, I cannot demonstrate the power of my words, but I have such a skill with playing words in my mother tongue that I can motivate or demotivate people, twist and turn the facts and influence the crowd effortlessly. Sometimes, this skill invites trouble too. When I was a tutor, many of my underperforming students achieved A, but they also mentioned that I hit and hurt their ego. As a result, they work hard to prove themselves. That's good; that was my intention. You need to know which style to use differently; the same ways do not work for everyone. When you are accomplished in this art, you will understand the best way to get the best results. Words themselves do not have power unless someone understands and takes them seriously. I bet none of you gets mad if I curse you in my language with a smile. Unless the person is receiving or understanding it, a word coming out of the mouth is just a nonsense sound. Thus, you should realize that selecting some specific terms and their delivery process can really turn a lifeless sentence into a magical weapon. I have won so many fights without fighting by using verbal strength. I will discuss how I used lingual strength to defeat my adversaries in chapter VIII, The Courage. If you practice playing with the best words to define a person you are conversing with, you can influence them so quickly. I have so many experiences regarding this. People around us are emotionally weak; you could be one of them. You chose a change, and change will indeed happen.

Emotional Strength

Things come and go. People are born and die. Nothing is permanent, including the hardship we go through. Even the darkest cloud has a silver lining; there is no such good or bad, but of course, divine and evil. Controlling emotions is not good at all, and getting influenced by them is even worse. In meditation practice, there is a term called 'Drashta Bhava' that means audience mind/feeling. Watch everything around you, soothing or disturbing; if you cannot control the situation by all means, just move forward. You do not need to blame yourself for something that is out of your hand. Don't be emotionally naïve, or you will be abused. People cut straight trees first in the wood. Similarly, people around you will misuse and abuse you if you are that straightforward. So, learn to be harsh sometimes. Let's discuss Drashta Bhava briefly because I like you to understand this and practice this in your daily life as much as possible.

When you are an audience in a theater, you watch plays but do not take any action. I mean, you see an antagonist murdering the innocents. You do not jump on the stage and fight with the antagonist. You will have the emotions and empathy towards the dying one, but you do not take any actions; this is called being 'drashta,' and the feelings that arise during that moment are bhava. That was an example of a theater. We can see examples in our daily life as well. Let's say you are thirsty right now. As a drashta, you would say that you are observing your thirst. You know the reasons and outcomes of it. Still, do not get panicked unless it is life-threatening. The main idea of having drashta bhava is to eliminate the emotional weakness that we have. When we are driven by our unrestrained emotions, we lose peace of mind, and when one makes decisions for peace of mind, we invite blunders. Never make any decisions for peace of mind. Instead, do it with peace of mind. When you look at everything as an audience, the panic mode of the brain shuts down. You may still have emotions, but you will have a peaceful mind to investigate the situation more. To carry out this principle in daily life is not easy. How can you watch yourself as an audience while somebody is kicking your bottom? I am telling you to be observant and not to panic in any situation. I never told you not to take appropriate action. If somebody is mistreating you or somebody else, do not watch and enjoy as an audience. I will discuss this topic more in chapter VIII, The Courage.

Drashta bhava is the beginning point of Gyan yoga; withouthaving this bhava, you cannot move forward in Gyan yoga. The objective of practicing Gyan yoga is to become a drashta. If you read Bhagwat Geeta, a must-read book, you get the idea about karma which means action. There are two terms related to all actions; Karta means performer or who does, and bhokta means enjoyer. When you are drashta, you observe your activities and all the enjoyments and cravings you have.

According to the Vedanta (Eastern Hindu philosophy), I enjoyed reading them and recommend everyone to read them. There are 4 significant margas, which means paths, to attain the higher consciousness. They are:

1. Gyan yoga, the path of wisdom and knowledge,
2. Bhakti yoga, the path of devotion,
3. Karma yoga, the path of selfless action and service, and
4. Raja yoga/ Dhyana yoga, the path of self-discipline and meditation.

All of these paths are equally effective, and they are independent of each other. I mean, you do not need to master all of them for salvation; only one is considered to be enough for achieving moksha. I have found knowledge of all of the above paths in Bhagawat Geeta. If you read it, you do not need to read many books. This chapter aims not to enlighten you with profound information about a different form of yoga. I would like you to detach from unnecessary attachments that you have made with many things around you. When you have some emotional thoughts coming into your mind, observe them. Enjoy it if it is a pleasant one and find its root if it is a painful one. If there is no way to fix the situation, move on. When something unpleasant happens through you, remember that you are not the one doing it; you are only a medium.

Thus, do not panic and observe everything as if you are watching a movie. Take a neutral side as much as possible to avoid being biased.

Behavioral Strength

Your actions should speak louder than words, and your character should be above all. When somebody trusts you, don't let them down. These are the more minor things we need to think about to purify ourselves from negativity. When your character is questionable, your conscious mind is more active as its function is to protect the subconscious mind. When you deviate from your 'Dharma,' means fundamental characteristic as human, your conscious mind may go through an identity crisis. If you are more destructive than constructive, evil than good, and dangerous than auspicious, your conscious mind accepts you as a negative character and informs the subconscious mind to attract unpleasant things towards you. The saddest part here is you will still love that since you are vibrating in a negative energy zone and anything that has a similar frequency, you attract them, and you love them. Don't you see in the news that terrorist slits throats of innocents and enjoys the moment? Can you and me do that? I even cannot imagine such a disturbing scene. No, we do not want that; nobody should follow such a detestable path. When someone calls you brother and you accepted it, stay like brother till the last breath. Don't stab on someone's back; no gossiping either. Maintain your character so strong that people can blindly trust you for who you are. When I was a teenager, my friends used to use my name to get away from their parents' scolding. Whenever they did a late-night party, they told their parents that they were with me until one day one of my friend's mothers asked me if they were with me, but I was completely unknown by the fact, and I told the truth. My impression of my hometown is pretty solid, and that is because of my understanding of behavioral strength. I want you to understand that everything we do, minor to major, has some impact on our behavior. When you are weak in this aspect, no one trusts you. Be trustworthy and never break it.

Flexibility

There are so many health issues we encounter as we get older, and decreasing in the ability to move joints through a complete range of motion, known as flexibility, is one of the significant issues. The joint issue is associated with aging so much that almost all elderly people suffer from it. Nearly all victims of this discomfort cannot run, walk up the stairs or stand for long. Maybe just ten years before, they could do all activities without any pain. If those elderly people who cannot walk start running suddenly and doing everything effortlessly, would you say that they are as healthy as they were ten years ago? Of course, yes. Can we say that their body reversed aging by ten years? Theoretically, yes, when we compare the body movements and activities before and after, the body has gone through reverse aging. But is it possible to reverse aging? Hypothetically, yes, but practically, we do not know many of the body activities that happen within us. If we do not see how it is happening, then reversing any process is not possible. While talking about the movability of the joints, we know the cause and method of the decline of its movability, and thus, we can reverse it. If we bring the movability of joints and muscles back in elderly people, won't they look younger and live longer? I think so. March 1st, 2005, the research was carried out by Dr. Anthony A. Vandervoort and the team on 'Geriatric fitness: Effects of aging and recommendations for exercise in older adults.' The research team designed an exercise program that included stretching exercises as part of the flexibility program and was reinforced to perform 2 to 3 or more days per week. Any type of flexibility activities such as yoga, Tai Chi, calisthenics, and Pilates were suggested (Vandervoort et al., 2005). The conclusion they got from their research in their own words are: "(1) exercise as an intervention is useful for maintaining and optimizing the components of fitness in older adults; (2) musculoskeletal function is improved with a balanced program of cardiorespiratory, resistance training, and flexibility activities; (3) older adults who have remained physically active do not undergo a decline in fitness to the same extent as those who have been inactive; and (4) despite aging, older adults can experience adaptation to exercise like that of younger adults (Vandervoort et al., 2005)."

If I can do all the physical activities that I used to do 10 years ago at the same level, I would definitely consider myself ten years younger. One flexibility practice I especially like to do every day is bending over and touching my toes without bending knees. If you can touch your toes in that manner, your muscles, joints, and tendons are early twenty years of age. You can sit and try to touch toes with a straight knee. Also, bend back and touch your knee or thigh with your forehead; you will be more flexible. This activity is for those who never stretch or do any flexibility activities.

Summary Of Chapter II

We need to be strong in so many aspects of life. Physical strength is the most vital one, but nothing else can be ignored. Being educated is not a big part of sharing knowledge; to be wise is the core intention. Be mindful all the time. Do not compromise with your character but do not get scared of change: the change is inevitable. Build muscles and maintain the right amount of fat. Performing any flexibility activities mentioned above won't take all day; do at least three repetitions. Play chess games on-line with the real opponent daily, at least three 10-minute games. Involve drashta bhava as much as possible in your daily activities. Every chapter of this book is dedicated to enhancing your power but not bringing a new personality that is not in you. You all are different from one another, and no one can replace each other. I want to remind you that no one can take your position and perform the duties; you are the only one specifically created for the specific job. You are the chosen one. Come on! Wake up, feel your responsibility and find the purpose of you being you.

By the end of the session (you need to practice all chapters for two and half months, as mentioned earlier), you will get closer to knowing yourself. I am adding some more activities to the schedule I created in the last chapter. Be mindful that as we go further in the books, the list of activities keeps changing; adding or subtracting will happen. The schedule can be switched based on the requirement, but actions must be the same. Otherwise, I cannot guarantee your spiritual and mundane-life success.

1. **Wake-up time: 6 A.M.**
2. **Drink water, sip by sip.**
3. **Write dream tracking journal.**
4. **Drink the boiled water with my recipe.**
5. **Practice deep breathing in an open area.**
6. **Chant the mantra you created.**
7. **Physical exercise, flexibility, and Chess game**
8. **Practice visualization (does not have to be in the morning).**
9. **Be kind all day.**
10. **Eat healthy.**
11. **Chant the mantra you created before bed.**

If you are a busy person, you do not need to spend too much time on every activity. However, your busy schedule cannot replace any of the activities. We all have 24 hours. If you do not have time, sacrifice something that is least important to you and find a room for these activities. At least, try for two and half months and see the magic.

CHAPTER III

ENHANCING WILLPOWER

There is no great talent without great willpower."
- Honore de Balzac

When I was learning Hypnosis in the early 2000s, I could not hypnotize the subject effectively. I was young and just approaching to the teenage phase. Thus, my conscious mind was restless and more argumentative. My centration was breaking. My guru observed my aura and realized that my willpower was getting so weak because of growing materialistic desires. I did not have doubts about the path I was getting in, but the children of the same age were seemed to have more fun than me. I had to be in strict discipline, quit eating meat, became a strict vegetarian, could not touch females except mother and sister while performing certain rituals and woke up early every day for pranayama and meditation. It seemed like I had a tough childhood because of spiritual practices, but it was a lot of fun for me. As I was progressing in spirituality, my ability to attract wealth and the people became powerful. However, it took me 20 years to realize being wealthy is not evil. We will discuss in detail the wealth in Chapter VII, The Wealth. This chapter is about willpower, and let's focus on it.

According to the Oxford dictionary, willpower can control your thoughts and actions to achieve what you want to do. In spirituality, we have a deeper understanding of it. In the meditation, it is known as *ICHHA SHAKTI*, and in Sadhana, it is called Sankalpa. Where there is *SANKALPA* (desires), there are two chances: Either Prāpti (obtained; fulfillment of wants) or Aprapti (unfulfillment of desires). In other words, Sankalpa is the cause, and Prāpti is the effect of Sankalpa. Prāpti is one of the Astha Siddhis (8 supernatural powers) in Yoga. Just for your information, I will put all info together here about those astha siddhis, but you do not need to get enticed by it and start practicing some weird techniques from YouTube.

8 supernatural powers I was talking about are:

- Aṇimā: Ability to reduce one's size, becoming smaller than an atom.
- Mahima: Ability to increase one's size.
- Garima: Ability to increase one's weight infinitely.
- Laghima: Ability to become lighter.
- Prāpti: Ability to Obtain anything upon will.
- Prākāmya: Ability to acquire anything one desired.
- Iṣiṭva: Lordship over creation
- Vaśitva: Having control over things

In Bhagwat Geeta, it is written Prāpti as follows:

Yatha Sankalpa samsiddhih means achieving as one determines.

Siddhi has a simple meaning, and it is the attainment of knowledge.

Ways to achieve Siddhis:

In ***Patanjali Yoga Sutras IV*: 1**, he mentioned the ways to attain such powers:

Yoga Sutra Chapter IV: Verse one

Janma ausadhi mantra tapah samadhijah siddhayah

MEANS: by- **Birth, medicine (drugs or herbs), mantra incantations, penance (self-discipline) and *Samadhi*.**

i) Birth: Some people are spiritually advanced. They follow dharma throughout their lives, and the baby they give birth has a high chance of receiving the powers through birth. Because of the righteous womb and the spiritual lifestyle of the parents, the baby is most likely to receive powers from the genes. A baby can also have a superpower from birth as per the attainments of his previous life.

ii) Medicine: Ancient text of the medicine, *Ayurveda*, explains how herbs can open up energy tunnels and activate the chakras. We know *Sanjeevani Boti*, a plant that had the power to bring the dead to life. The name of the plant was mentioned in the Hindu textbook, Ramayana. Likewise, Ayurveda talks about thousands of other herbs that are very rare for present days. However, to achieve such powers through herbs is absolutely possible.

iii) *Mantra* (Incantations): Mantra itself is a science. We all know in the beginning there was a sound. So, the incantation is a way to produce a sound that resonance with our internal humming sound. Vedas are full of mantras. During those days, people were very disciplined, and most of the time would be spent on this incantation practice. Mantras are also widely used in Sadhanas. Now, *Sadhana* is a different topic. It includes Tantra, Mantra, and Yantra. Chanting the same word several thousand times in a particular manner would give a high concentration power, and automatically an individual would start vibrating in such a frequency that he would attain supernatural powers. Chanting mantras has to be done by following several rules and procedures.

iv) Self-Discipline: Why do we need to be self-disciplined? This is only the way to clear the mind. How to clear the mind? The answer is very straightforward; controlling over five senses organs through which we collect infinite information. By controlling the senses, Clear the mind to have control over five elements that we are made up of. Changing your body temperature, making yourself light, and so on.

v) Samadhi: When someone achieves oneness with higher consciousness, he will access the supernatural powers. This is the 8th and the last part of Yoga, according to the Patanjali. Some people can experience Samadhi without completing the other seven stages; it could be by accident or birth. However, to achieve Samadhi is not a piece of cake. You can understand the degree of its difficulty by studying the life of Siddhartha Gautam Buddha; how hard it was for him to attain Nirvana, Samadhi.

So, coming back to willpower again. We struggle every day to achieve goals in our lives, and many a time, we still fail to grab them. We blame everything and everyone, but we always forget to see the root cause of the problems. When we are not persistent in achieving our goals, we get distracted by failures. Our willpower gets weaken when we give up on our dreams.

Some people and psychology experts believe that willpower is just like a muscle that can get fatigued from overuse. I am firmly against it. Self-control indeed is one of the vital components that build willpower, and a person may get tired of self-restraint and discipline in the long run. As a result, willpower breaks, and a person gives up on his dream. For example, if you use willpower to work hard to buy a house. You will work harder and still do not feel like you actually did it. You don't get low in morale while doing so because of the effect of willpower; you will be motivated until you get what you want. Experts believe that your willpower may get fatigued once you have the house and less effective for other goals, which is not valid. First of all, willpower cannot be compared with physical things such as muscles that get fatigued. Willpower is the combination of words that motivates a person from a subconscious level. When a message is passed to the subconscious mind, you do not need to worry about willpower depletion. On June 9th, 2015, a research journal was published by

Thomas de Haan and Roel van Veldhuizen on 'Willpower depletion and framing effects.' "Our view is that the fact that we do not find any effect of willpower depletion across several tasks in three experiments suggests that the effects of willpower depletion in general and specifically in the Stroop task may not be as consistent and strong as the existing psychological literature suggests (Haan et al.,2015)" I wrote exactly what they found in their finding, word by word. There is no proof and evidence of depletion of willpower due to overuse. You do not need to worry about the rumours. The experiences I am sharing are being passed on from person to person for several millennia. Strong willpower also keeps us healthy. It frees us from anxiety and depression. To vibrate at a positive energy level, willpower plays a crucial role. The research was carried out on 'The effect of willpower workshop on anxiety, depression, and the excitement components in the students of Shiraz University of medical sciences' by Seyed Ziaeddin Tabei and team on January 1st, 2019. The research indicated that willpower plays an essential role in making sound mental health. The result of the study showed a significant positive correlation between the use of willpower techniques and the promotion of an individual's mental health (Tabei et al., 2019).

It is effortless to fall back rather than climbing up in the energy pyramid. How much effort you can put to stand back and how much pain you can withstand signify your willpower level. There are infinite ways to strengthen willpower, so does it to weaken it. I will discuss some of them that I found easy to stick with.

Not Breaking A Promise

For most of us, breaking promises is a regular thing. The impact of those activities on our conscious and subconscious minds is tremendous. When we repeat such activities several times, it becomes our habit, and there is no control of the conscious mind over our addiction. That means actions that have become your habit are in auto-pilot mode. What do you understand from this? Yes, patterns are driven by the subconscious mind. This is why it is so difficult to get rid of smoking, drinking, and any other activities that have become our habits. We form patterns only when our conscious mind accepts them as an essential activity of life. The repetition, feelings, and enjoyment of the action are some elements that help us fool our conscious mind into making it believe that we need those activities to survive. According to the author of the book 'The Power of Habit,' Charles Duhigg, a habit can be broken down into three parts to understand: the first part of habit is the cue. It is a kind of trigger that tells your conscious mind to awake sub-conscious mode and let a behavior unfold (Duhigg, radio broadcast, 2012) and then the routine and repetition of the action. The last part of it is the reward. Whenever the action is completed, the brain releases happy hormones, dopamine. Now, because the body has just experienced a nice feeling, the conscious mind believes the activity is an auspicious one and helps build a more profound connection with the subconscious mind. In this way, we become the victim of all bad habits. If you keep on breaking promises, first of all, you will lose the trust of people. We can see it physically, and it does not need proof either. Most of the time, people make so many promises to themselves and barely fulfill all. When breaking promises continue for an extended period, you will make a habit out of it, resulting in feeble willpower. Willpower is concerned with making goals and achieving them in the desired time, but you will procrastinate and never meet your deadline when you cannot keep promises. Then, consecutive failures will knock at your door, and after seeing so much failure in life, you will lose hope. You can only go downwards in the energy pyramid with this kind of dirty energy and vibration. There is no other thing that can motivate us as well as our own success. Many people may believe that failure is the primary source of the motivation for success; they are hallucinating. Failure itself is negative energy and vibrating in depressive mode. A negatively charged energy either sucks your positivity or converts you into a hostile entity. Thus, a successful person always fights it but never accepts failure. Be a magnet of success. If you want to bring positivity to your life, add energy to your aura, you must think and do positive things. If you promise someone to take care of her and that is only the promise you made to her, you need to fulfill it. There is one way to stay away from this effect of mental karma, and it is never to promise to anyone. When I pledged my guru not to eat meat, I never touched it. I promised a girl not to show my face again, I left the country. I promised myself not to indulge in alcohol; I hate the presence of it. I promised my mother to buy a house in Texas in 5 months, though I did not have a source of income, I accomplished it in 3 months. My friends and relative know the sturdiness of my words; never broke my promises. When you keep your promises and successfully accomplish them, the conscious mind believes that you are trustworthy and stops scrutinizing the thought you want to pass to the subconscious level. As a result, your words turn out into reality quickly. When you have to make any promises, think several times before you make any commitment and make yourself clear that you are fulfilling only the latest promise that you might have done several with a single individual. For example, you promised your girlfriend to be there in her life for her at any cause. After a few years, you are compelled to make another promise to leave her because of her choice; you are not guilty of it. Your conscious mind knows the situation. Be wise in wording a promise; think like a written contract between your conscious and subconscious mind. You need to word the contract in such a way that if you have to get out of it, you should be able to do it without a great deal of damage. For example, I promise that I will never leave you until you want me to. In this sentence, I have added a tail sentence, 'until you want me to.' This sentence gives you the freedom when the situation worsens between you two, and you will be vindicated, no doubt. Also, until you mention the phrase 'I promise that....', it won't be considered as a promise. It will be just a statement. You are not liable for any comments. Without having any commitments and promises, your willpower cannot grow stronger either. Thus, I do not advise you to not have obligations. You must have them. Start with the easier one and prove yourself with those beginning successful steps. Promise to go to the gym for a week; this is achievable. When you do it, challenge your willpower with additional activities. Slowly, you will see the effects; you will discover a new character thriving within you.

Guard Your Secret

What do you think is the greatest weakness of your life? Many answers love failure, wealth, family, and so on. The greatest weakness of our life is our secrets. Believe me or not, we all have some secrets. When you live in the illusion that sharing your all secrets makes you an open-hearted person, you are making a colossal blunder. I often hear people saying that their life is an open book, and they share everything they were not supposed to. I am not telling you to lie but telling the truth does not mean telling your secrets to everyone without any compulsion. You never know who turns their back and becomes your enemy in the future. When you trust someone and tell your secrets, later on, the same person uses your secrets to embarrass you and hurt you verbally or physically. There is a great epic known as Ramayana. In this historical event, Ram killed Ravana because Vibhishana, the younger brother of Ravana, betrayed his brother and shared his biggest secret. After knowing the secret of Ravana, Ram understood where to shoot the arrow, and thus, Ravana died. If Ravana had never told his brother about his secret, his brother would not pass it on to Ram, and today, probably, all of us would never know about Ram and would revere Ravana as a positive character because history is always written by winners. You came alone and will go alone even though two persons died hugging each other; this is inevitable. If something goes with you is the knowledge, experience, and the secret you never told anyone. All types of secrets are your weakness. It can be related to the job, business, and personal life. Keeping secrets and not telling the truth are different from one another. The former has to be done, and the latter should be avoided. When you hide something important about yourself, do not be suspicious, though. When I emphasize the secret, I mean life-threatening or life-changing information and other minor secrets that people do not necessarily need to know about you. Do not open your mouth to vomit your secret as soon as you feel the other person is trustworthy, not even your high school grades. It is up to you about what needs to be guarded and whatnot; just don't act weird anyway. My father often used to share his business ideas with everyone he thought could be trusted. As a result, his wealthy friend would start that business way before my dad would collect the capital. I have gone through several embarrassments just because of trusting someone and sharing my personal secret. If you think you are open, like I used to be, and there is nothing secret about you, then you do not know yourself well. Take a seat and think about the past. The biggest embarrassment you have experienced is because of you trusting others and sharing your weak points. Be present; only speak when required, answer when needed, and speak short and sweet about yourself. Let your character define you, not your words.

Being An Optimistic

No doubt, having a positive thought can bring calmness in our life. As a human, when something terrible happens, we tend to have tons of negative thoughts and emotions. We all have that tendency, but only a well-trained mind can see the positive part of it. When your house is on fire, what is the first thought? It is about the loss, economic loss. Everybody thinks that way; it is not possible to overcome that feeling. Have you ever noticed that a list of them follows you one after the other when one bad thing happens to you? Like, your vehicle breaks down on the way to work. The phone's network does not work while trying to contact your supervisor. You miss the client meeting and eventually get fired from the job. Then, you come back home and fight with your wife. The wife goes to her mom's house and so on and on. This is just an example of trying to show you a negative spiral that can be motivated by one negative thought. Thus, when something terrible happens, we should try to find the most prominent positive side. If my house is on fire, I will thank God for me not being inside the house. If my car breaks down on the way to work, I would not panic and feel good for not having any accidents. It is straightforward to imagine that we can find some positive reasons to stay positive, but in reality, if our mind is not well trained, the first thing we think will be negative. Just remember your past and ask yourself if I am not right. Our conscious mind is far more innovative than we know.

When we talk about the conscious mind, I feel a little dumb every time because we are trying to understand the conscious mind while staying at the conscious level. It's like I am talking about myself; if so, of course, I will speak what I want. Similarly, when the conscious mind explains what it is, it may not talk the whole truth, or it may guard its secret. Thus, to understand this level of mind, we need to stand on a different level of mind to see all aspects of the conscious mind. This is why we should listen to yogis, meditators, or philosophers as much as we can because they have seen the conscious mind from its upper level. How can just being positive help a person to feel good while something awful is happening? This seems impractical in some critical cases, such as somebody's death or when someone becomes the victim of rape. In such cases, no matter how ingenious and accomplished your mind is in positivity, you will constantly shift towards negative thoughts first. However, practicing positivity can break the cycle of inviting a series of evil fates towards us. Being optimistic not only has psychological effects on an individual but also has physical effects. According to the research of Zahra Nikmanesh and Linda Mirkazehi on July 1st, 2020 on 'Research paper: The effectiveness of positive thinking training in the quality of life and emotion regulation among patients with multiple sclerosis,' positive thinking has direct benefits to the mental and physical health of the patient. It is found that positive thinking creates a set of behaviors, hope, self-esteem, and self-confidence. Concerning the results of their study, researchers recommend conducting a positive thinking training program for patients, and they also think that everyone should be taught positive thinking skills as it promotes the quality of life of patients and helps them to regulate their emotions in a better way (Nikmanesh et al., 2020).

Patience

My understanding of patience and practice may be a lot different from yours. I consider it a big psychological dam that exists in my mind that stops the flow of all unwanted activities that are motivated and directed towards me to impair me. As a result, I am more tolerant. I actually have found myself more tolerant and easy-going than a lot of people I met. Some people have mentioned my high patience level as well. However, as I mentioned above, the psychological wall or dam in my mind is not infinitely tall and robust. Sooner or later, emotions, pains, and sufferings will crush the barrier, and I will lose patience. I think this is very dangerous, but in my experience, I have exploded only a few times, and I had no choice. I will discuss this further in chapter VIII: The Courage.

For me, the definition of patience is not limited to being able to wait long for something without complaint. It also means sticking with people or things by accepting a certain level of their influences. In a general sense, patience refers to a capability that allows a person to hold on to something for long. Thus, patience and an understanding of time may come together sometimes. Waiting for someone for long, hoping for a good result of the test, expecting someone's love, tolerating someone's abusive nature, holding some stocks and waiting for the best time to sell, and demonstrating the ability to be positive for an extended period. So, what is the relationship between patience and willpower, then? How patience influence will? Patience and willpower look different from each other because willpower motivates you to grab success whereas, patience tells you to wait for better. But in reality, our conscious mind is always inclined towards willpower. As a result, when there is potential pleasure and success, we move towards it. Another side of being patience is being strong on the mental level. The trick is here: when we have something desirable in front of us but control ourselves from grabbing it and waiting for a better version, there is some kind of resistance in mind. Something in us tells us to reach for the stuff, and at the same time, we push ourselves to wait.

Hypothetically, something here is getting stretched and compressed, respectively. It just works like a muscle fiber; when it is stretched and compressed with resistance, the thread breaks down and eventually generates more muscles fibers. Similarly, willpower extends our willingness to achieve something, and patience brings stretched willpower back to the place. As a result, willpower will attain a higher level of potential energy. Thus, patience eventually works for strengthening willpower though they are opposite to each other. For goals such as losing or gaining weight, having patience is everything. However, the driving force to achieve success is, undoubtedly, willpower. But if there is no patience in an individual, then willpower alone cannot accomplish the mission. In such activities, patience and willpower go along.

Perform 1% More Than It Demands

Everyone knows that we need to work harder to achieve anything we desire. Then why should I be reiterating the phrase? I need to repeat the importance of willpower, and you would not ignore it when you see it repeatedly. This is precisely similar to pushing yourself for an extra two repetitions in a set while working out. Though we already proved logically and experimentally that willpower is not like any muscle that gets fatigued after overuse, a similar explanation can be used to understand how willpower gets stronger with such diligence. Giving up means accepting failure or accepting oneself as not being worthy of something. Giving up on something may give us temporary happiness and benefits, but it makes us weak and lazy in the long run. It also promotes us to focus on plan B or C before working on A. When people know there is something to fall back on, they do not work hard. As a result, they fall back and feel happy because there were some backup plans. When we think about a backup plan, we are already sure we cannot do it but yet take a chance. You may get success by chance. But to stay in that position will be harder for you; success coming out of an opportunity does not last long.

On the contrary to this, if you do not plan on having a 'falling back plan,' you will do what it takes to succeed in the chosen field. Taking action has two outcomes: success or failure. Most people change their route and live with plan B when they fail twice or thrice on plan A. It is understandable to lose hope, but at least you tried thrice. How about trying some more attempts? Never know; the success is on the 4th trial. When you fail so many times, I bet you will have more knowledge than anybody who achieves grand success on it on his first trial. Just stick around with your dream; willpower will guide you through. Similarly, when we put 1% more effort into our dream, the feeling of exceeding in performing duty makes us optimistic about success. Every time we achieve more than we targeted, the success is very close. It is very similar in the business too. When someone exceeds the target of the month, he gets extra benefits from the company. Likewise, when we achieve additional success in exceeding our target, willpower gets more assertive, and the conscious mind offers us bonuses and benefits. Suppose you go to the gym to walk on the treadmill, walk for 10 min, and switch to run for 3 min. Continue this cycle for as long as you had planned the time for walking. I am sure you feel different this time. I do not want you to bring a drastic change overnight, but do something helpful for your dream in a small amount every day. When willpower is enhanced, you will see its magic; you will start having fun in the process of a dream come true. Nothing will discourage you. Above all, you will have strong willpower to alter the brain wave upon your will. So, don't underestimate your willpower.

Some other things that we need to be mindful of to strengthen willpower are:

1. Being truthful at any cost.
2. Being grateful.
3. Be responsible for one's words and actions.
4. Avoiding excuses.

All positive virtues that our conscious mind thinks are characteristics of a noble person, we should adhere to. Everything we are doing is to please our conscious mind to get the key to the subconscious level; at any cost, we will achieve success.

Summary Of Chapter III

I hope I have been able to inform you of something new about willpower. Trust me, these techniques seem to be easy but are very effective. I practice them in my daily life; if I can do it, you can do it too. I think you may get more benefits and reach your goal faster if you stick with them. Also, you may succeed in spirituality and get way deeper than me because we all are different, and some techniques that I discussed in this book are amazingly auspicious for some people that may expedite their spiritual journey. Even if you do not want to dive into spirituality, strengthening willpower will undoubtedly make your life healthy, wealthy, and successful. Most of the activities I gathered together in this chapter could be used as a source of information to boost up your motivation. However, you must carry out at least one activity in your schedule. Otherwise, I would feel like my research time and effort to bring a change has been wasted. But I know you will get motivated to see the world from a different point of view.

If you are not convinced with me for most of my reasoning, it is fine, but give it a try and see if I am right. If you think you do not have enough time to apply all principles from this chapter to your daily schedule, do not include all. However, use your sense and reasoning in selecting the most effective one. From this chapter, if only one thing I have to suggest to anyone regardless of their goal, whether spirituality or materialistic, I would advise guarding one's secret at all cost. But, simply being mindful of other ideas I discussed here would not hurt at all. Those who are planning to choose spirituality more should accept these techniques as principles for two and half months to open yourself for a more significant thing coming towards you. It is entirely upon you that how you want to set up your daily routine. Anyway, I will keep posting an example version of a daily routine as we complete the chapter (as I promised earlier).

1. **Wake-up: 6 A.M.**
2. **Drink water, sip by sip.**
3. **Write dream tracking journal.**
4. **Drink the boiled water with my recipe.**
5. **Practice deep breathing in an open area.**
6. **Chant the mantra you created.**
7. **Physical exercise, flexibility, and Chess game**
8. **Practice visualization (does not have to be in the morning).**
9. **Be kind, and practice the willpower in as many activities as possible.**
10. **Eat healthy.**
11. **Chant the mantra you created before bed.**

CHAPTER IV

CELIBACY

"Celibacy goes deeper than the flesh."- F. Scott Fitzgerlad

In the beginning, I was thinking about putting celibacy under the chapter of willpower because the most vital force that strengthens our willpower is celibacy. There are no other practices and techniques as powerful as this to enhance willpower. Then, I realized that this topic is ambiguous and will require a lot of information from biology and spirituality to explain its importance. Thus, I decided to create a separate chapter to discuss where I will talk about it only, and I think this topic deserves particular attention.

Celibacy means abstaining from having sex or similar activities and staying away from such thoughts and imagination. Some people even take it to the next level by detaching themselves from all kinds of attachments to the world. For them, getting attached to materials is also involving in some way of sex. I am not going to cover those principles here. My reasoning in this chapter is based on the scientific facts from organismal biology. However, I will not provide solid proof for some specific phenomena I will talk about in this chapter. I will share my experiences of it as well as some other peoples'.

I do not recommend any ordinary person to practice celibacy

longer than a month as it has a tendency to make you happier without involving in such activities, and you may never marry. Practicing abstinence, a week or ten days will definitely promote emotional and physical health. The most prolonged practice I have ever done is two years, from Dec 2010 to Jan 2013. Some people have practiced this for their entire life, as they claimed. A great personality such as Vivekananda went celibacy for an extended period, and it is recorded that he had a photographic memory, could read hundreds of pages in 30 min and remember everything. He was not bright and genius like that before he accepted spirituality and celibacy. He candidly gave credit to his ability to practice self-denial. He also said that if anyone practices celibacy from mind and body for ten years, he will achieve tremendous mental agility. If you practice virtue for this long, you will not return to the material world, I guarantee it. Practicing celibacy is not easy at all. Even if you successfully save your sperms during the day, it will surely fall at night because you can control your conscious mind by reasoning but not the subconscious mind. A research journal 2017 on 'Commitment to celibacy in German catholic priests' was published on January 1st by Klaus Baumann and team. The research found that it was highly stressful for 75% of priests (out of 2549 priests who participated in the study) to tackle the problems associated with celibate life (Baumann et al., 2017). According to the journal, in its own words, "Commitment to celibacy is a complex matter influenced by various more or less "facilitating" external factors and sociocultural environments as well as individual dispositions, attitudes, and behaviours, including spiritual convictions, values, and related practices." Thus, if there is no strong motivation for it, you will never be able to persist in the practice of celibacy. According to an article, 'The power of Celibacy: An experience beyond the senses,' published in August 2007 by Riveros, the practice of celibacy provides a great deal of physical strength, stamina, and increment in muscle quality. "Your mind will be sharper and acute. You will be able to understand subtleties. Your intellect will be deep and broad." He spoke.

We can read hundreds of experiences explaining celibacy's power, but there is no excellent and tangible way through which we can actually see the effects without practicing it. We still cannot imagine how it works. I have tried to understand it based on my experiences and the scientific knowledge I have, along with all means, including research papers. It will be more intense for those who do not like science and reasoning. I have tried to explain every minor detail as I can to make my imagination clear. I hope you will find it easy to understand and you will enjoy it.

Several powerful forces naturally exist in the universe. Sex is one of the most vital energies necessary for evolution because it brings ***genetic variability***. On the other hand, there is ***asexual reproduction*** where there is no need for two parents and no ***gamete*** formation occurs. Since everyone has an identical DNA copy, the disease may affect all the individuals, and the whole population may extinct if the environment is not favourable. Most simpler organisms, such as amoeba, bacteria, hydra, and some plants, reproduce via the asexual method, whereas all multicellular and complex organisms such as birds, cats, dogs, cows, humans, etc. a partner for reproduction. It is incredible that no organism (healthy and normal) ever had to learn about sex; this is the built-in system nature has installed inside each living organism's DNA. When the gametes (sperm in male and ova or eggs in female) are formed, the opposite sexes are attracted. There is a special force that brings two individuals together for reproduction.

Many people confuse this force as love, but love and sex are different in fundamental ways. What is the difference between the love of a father and that of a husband for a girl? Both males love the girl so much. In fact, the father has loved the girl for decades. However, the girl will pick the other man she has been dating, maybe, only for a few months. If the love is identical, why doesn't she stay with her father? Also, she knows her father from the soul; however, she picks other men because of an undefined force urging her to decide. Simply, there is something within us that motivates us to have sex and reproduce. What if we deny getting inspired for sex and follow the path of celibacy?

By accepting celibacy, by default, you are going against nature. It is like throwing a ball vertically upward against gravity to0 many of us. However, if one tries, this is not impossible.

How *Celibacy* Works

So that you will understand this in a better way, I give you an example. Assume that you were building a house. You hired, let say, 15 labours for it by paying them daily, and they were very hard working too. They spent all day building four walls on the ground level and then left to come the next day. Unfortunately, some bad people in the neighbourhood stole all the bricks by breaking the walls at night.

The next day, you went to the site with workers to see no walls. You did not have any choice but to rebuild the walls. You spent another day and extra money to pay for the workers. At night, thieves came and stole bricks again.

In the morning, you went there with workers and rebuild the wall.

The same thing happened again and again. You never tried to solve the problem effectively. Workers were making money every day. So, they don't have a problem with thieves, but you were getting nothing. Not even a single wall was completed. In this way, you would never have a complete house.

SIMILARLY,(images on page 63 & 64)

After a certain age, meiosis cell division takes place for the formation of gametes. The organs such as the testes and ovaries get busy in this process. There are two stages **of Meiosis (I** and **II)** consisting of other phases. In each step and phase of a cell division, while copying the chromosome in **Meiosis I** and chromatid in II, while the spindles are forming, while chromosomes and chromatids move towards the different locations within the cell, there is an involvement of an undefined force, which is obviously, fuelled by the combustion of food we take. So, just to form a single sperm**(** gamete), a cell must undergo a complex and well-designed (seem to be) process.

One-half of duplicated chromosomes are called chromatids. Each chromatid contains a cap structure called a telomere. In both *Meiosis* (in gamete formation) and mitosis (in other cell divisions such as skin, nails, etc. other than gametes), the telomere length is shortened after each division.

The telomere's function is to ensure that there is no too much genetic information lost each time cell division occurs. When a minimum amount of remaining genetic information is reached, the telomere is almost lost. This shortened telomere prevents the cells from replicating more. We lose telomere as we get older because we undergo several cell divisions throughout life.

There Are Two Hypothetical Ways To Prevent Excessive Unwanted Cell Division

1. Stay healthy so that our system does not have to undergo mitosis to replace our non-functioning cells.

2. Stop wasting too many gametes.

Understanding in-depth, celibacy is less related to the production of gametes, sperms, or eggs. The main thing associated with it is the sexual fluid released from both males' and females' reproductive organs when they are experiencing orgasm. So, the juice related to the orgasm has to be protected. Don't you feel weak after orgasm?

Again, coming back to the example of building a house- if the bricks are not stolen, workers will complete the walls. Then, you can make them work on the roof or so on.

In the example, the workers are used to illustrate the internal systems or organs that produce gametes. The money given to them is energy provided to the system, and the example of bricks is a metaphor for the release of sexual fluids and gamete during orgasm.

When there is abstinence from sex or masturbation, our inner system will provoke us for sex after one time. We become even more sexual during this celibacy time. If we force ourselves to remain calm and stay away from orgasm, we will dream of having it, and we release fluid. Once you release liquid, knowingly or unknowingly, you break the rule, and then your tank is empty. Your inner system will again be busy making gametes and fluids, which will consume time and cellular energy.

But let's say you succeed in controlling emotions and stopping the release. Since you are fighting against nature, it will try several ways to abet you to follow its reproduction rule. The first step of your system is to stimulate the Swadhisthana Chakra. The sudden change in the behaviour of Swadhisthana can make a person hypersexual. Now, s/he does not have a choice but release the fluid. But a meditation sadhaka has a way to control it. Many practitioners believe that sperm moves upward through the spine, which helps in kundalini awakening, but this is not true. In reality, not the sperm or fluid but the cell's energy used for the cell division and the gamete formation is moving upwards. In the example, you are not taking the same bricks to construct the roof. Since you were not losing the bricks, you used that money for the roofing materials.

Yogis can experience kundalini awakening without practicing celibacy. However, they have to be in a meditative state all the time to access the energy. But, for the yogi who has practiced abstinence, he has the power preserved inside. As a result, he accesses it at any time.

If you don't ejaculate for years, not even in the dream (no night falls), sex; a powerful force, will be converted into potential energy inside your body which can be used in any form (memory, vision, intuition, physical strength, strengthen the immune, etc. at any time and whenever you want.

In points, I will put the outcomes of celibacy as:

1. Celibacy preserves cellular energy.

2. However, celibacy does not guarantee a long life because the telomere is shortened by mitosis cell division.

3. The brain will get more energy. As a result, memory power will be immense.

4. A person will be more mindful as well as an increment in physical strength.

5. More creative. And so on.

That was my understanding of how celibacy works on our bodies. I may be wrong on my reasoning part for this chapter, but I am not inappropriate for telling you its benefits because there are real advantages of practicing it from mind and body. It not only enhances willpower but also boosts your energy level. With the help of this activity, you can get rid of your mental weakness and jump to the upper level of the energy pyramid.

The picture of cell divisions we talked on page 60 is as follows:

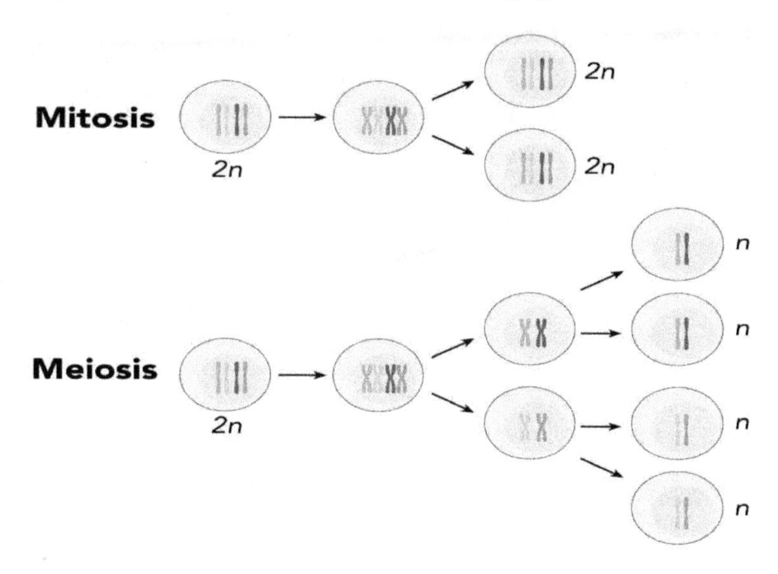

Summary Of Chapter IV

Though it is challenging to follow and highly impossible to explain its function and process, celibacy is a widely accepted fact that brings well-being. All major religions took it as the best and shortcut way to reach to the god. This practice will not only strengthen our willpower but also purify us from mental junk. There is no doubt that practicing it gives us physical and psychological strength. I have experienced this in my life. The learning capability will skyrocket, and memory power will be excellent. Our goal in this book to discuss celibacy is not to be a monk; we are enhancing willpower. You can practice celibacy for a week in a month or a month in a year. The longer you go, the lesser your desire for sex will be. If you do not pursue a saint life, I would not suggest you go for longer than a month in a row. Put your mind and body on one point; do with your heart if you want to do it; otherwise, just don't try because there will be no appeasing result for the mediocre trials.

The picture of telomere that gets shortens after each cell division as discussed on page 60 is as below.

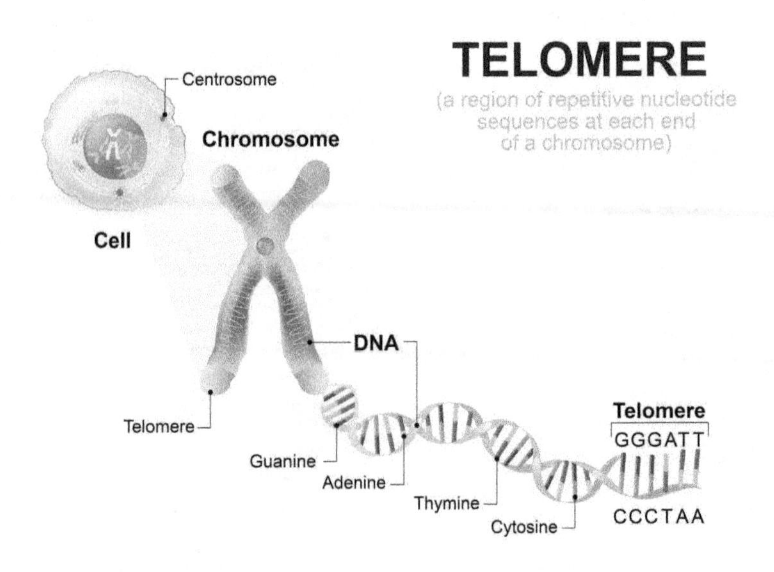

1. **Wake-up: 6 A.M.**
2. **Drink water, sip by sip.**
3. **Write dream tracking journal.**
4. **Drink the boiled water with my recipe.**
5. **Practice deep breathing in an open area.**
6. **Chant the mantra you created.**
7. **Physical exercise, flexibility, and Chess game**
8. **Practice visualization (does not have to be in the morning).**
9. **Be kind, and practice the willpower in as many activities as possible.**
10. **Eat healthy and detach yourself from unnecessary desires.**

1. Chant the mantra you created before bed.

CHAPTER V

THE PURPOSE

"Your purpose in life is to find your purpose and give your whole heart and soul to it."- Buddha

Look around. We are surrounded by hundreds of different devices and equipment. From a pen to a toaster, we cannot live happily without any devices we are surrounded with. When we observe them carefully, we understand that everything has been created for some reason; all of them have a purpose of fulfilling. Like a pen is designed to write and a toaster is to toast the bread. If they want to trade or quit their purpose and function, we will have difficulty living our lives. Thank God that everything is not conscious at the same level.

Nothing in the universe is entirely useless or a complete waste. The thing which is unnecessary for one could be essential for others. It's not only about the point of view of one another either. Actually, it's the fact that the purpose of one device cannot fulfill that of another unless the creator has created such a multipurpose device, which is possible. My point is when we realize the primary purpose of things around us, living our life would be a lot easier. In this high-tech world, we know the purpose of almost everything around us though we use or misuse them. If I ask anyone about the purpose of a telephone, none will miss the correct answer. Even a kid of six years old can answer it.

We are so much educated about the external world, there is no doubt.

We created so many things to make our life easier. We could not walk all day, so we devised vehicles. We want appeasing weather throughout the year, which is not possible worldwide, so we created fans and air conditions. We hate darkness, so we made a lightbulb. We like to be connected with our people though we are far away from them, so we created social media. So many things we have made today; amazingly, we know their fundamental purposes. But, how about you and your life? Do you know your purpose?

When we talk about the purpose of life, there are two groups of people. One believes in creation, the religious-minded, and another, the scientific-minded, in evolution. The theory of creation in various religions is varied. Besides, they disagree with each other. As a result, the first group is divided into several pieces itself. Whereas the group that believes in evolution seems to be unified since their belief system is the science that is the same. Though there are disagreements in the creation process in all religions, the source of the creation and the creator is omniscient, omnipotent, and omnipresent. All religious people believe that there is someone who created us and takes care of us. On the other hand, evolution does not suggest that someone created us and saves us from danger. These are the topics we can argue all day and night; we still fail to come to a conclusion. From the biography of Albert Einstein, Sir Isaac Newton, Blaise Pascal, Erwin Schrodinger, Gregor Mendel, Guglielmo Marconi, James Clerk Maxwell, Johannes Kepler, Louis Pasteur, Max Planck, Michael Faraday, Nicholas Copernicus, Rene Descartes, Robert Boyle, Robert A. Millikan, Werner Heisenberg, William Thomson Kelvin and from the work of many other iconic scientists it is found that they believed in creator. An Indian genius and mathematician named Ramanujan (1887-1920) contributed to the theory of numbers and pioneered the discoveries of the properties of the partition function. He accepted that the source of his mathematical knowledge was one of the Hindu Goddess called Namagiri Thayar. He said, "An equation for me is meaningless unless it expresses a thought of God." If you do not know about him, search on google, you will be surprised.

Usually, while talking about evolution in general, we only talk about the process that might have occurred to the monkeys to transform into humans. But the evolution is not limited to any animal kingdom. Everything must have evolved, and if we can track down the process in reverse order, we may be able to see who came from what. We cannot go back in time physically yet, but our imagination can. However, we need plenty of facts from today to imagine what might have happened in the course of the evolution. Let's do some fiction.

While doing research on life, I came across a video of Ted-Ed. I found it interesting to share it here. It goes like this:

Life began from the chemical combination of information molecules when they started to reproduce and evolve by natural selection. A single-cell bacterium called Cyanobacteria is the main reason for the complex life like us. Three and half billion years ago, the earth's atmosphere was mostly Nitrogen, Carbon dioxide, and Methane. All oxygen atoms were locked up with water, and the oceans were populated by anaerobic microbes. They are unicellular organisms that thrive in the absence of oxygen. In between 2 to 3.5 billion years ago, some of these anaerobic microbes began to float on the ocean's surface, which caused an evolution of a new ability known as photosynthesis. Now, they can produce energy by themselves by using sunlight, and the population of these bacteria multiplies rapidly. They started polluting the atmosphere by producing oxygen as the byproduct of photosynthesis. In the beginning, all of the oxygen was absorbed in rusting due to a chemical reaction with iron. But after several hundred million years, the population of Cyanobacteria produced much more oxygen than it was consumed in the chemical reaction. The oxygen gas started accumulating in the atmosphere of the earth. But this was not good for other organisms because the oxygen-rich atmosphere was toxic to them. As a result, 2 billion years ago, all life extinct except Cyanobacteria and some other species. This event is called The Oxygen Catastrophe Event.

Earlier, when there was no oxygen, methane was trapping the heat, making the earth warm. Still, plenty of oxygen reacted with methane to produce Carbon dioxide and water, making the atmosphere lighter and cooler. Now, the environment of the earth was suitable for the mutation of the bacteria. Hundreds of million years ago, some other prehistoric species of bacteria engulfed cyanobacteria which are called endosymbiosis. That microbe now had its own internal energy-generating part within itself, which was cyanobacteria. Later on, cyanobacteria became the chloroplast of the organism, and the cell became the ancestor of the plant cell. Similarly, several diversities of life existed after several mutations.

On February 14th, 2021, a research journal was published on 'Molecules, information and the origin of life: What is next?' by Salvatore Chirumbolo and Antonio Vella. In conclusion, the authors said, "In recent years, many fundamental theories have been reported, and probably life emerged not merely by the random ability of chance and the mandatory pulse of necessity but by dissipative mechanisms, where probably information and thermodynamics are closely intertwined in a chaotic dynamic ultimately held by water." We can simply understand in our words that life has emerged as a chemical-physical dissipative system, where minerals, clays, water started the first catalytic reactions following other processes to form a complex biology system (Chirumbolo et al., 2021).

It is mindboggling to imagine that something extremely complex like us once originated from chemical compounds with the ability to replicate themselves along with their specific information. Who put the information in them? How could a chemical compound such as CH_4, for example, present in ancient times, decide to pass on their information after multiplying themselves? Why did not everything turn into biological components? It seems like everything was a deliberately carried out plan. Somebody put consciousness inside the compounds and sat behind to see the consequences.

As time passed, several species of organisms, from bacteria to whales, formed. Believing this philosophy, I firmly believe in evolution created by the creator. My understanding of God is not similar to the concept of any religion. Anyway, I will use the term God to refer to the creator.

In the above excerpt, I talked about the creator, God, and the creation, conscious chemical compounds. Now, coming back to the point that we were trying to understand the word 'purpose' of our life. Following paragraphs are my ways to see life, and the philosophy I am explaining is solely based on my experience and thought process. You do not necessarily have to agree with me. However, I really do not want you to completely disagree because I want you to have a purposeful and happy life. If you do not believe in the philosophy behind creating something, you may not find any motivation to give a good direction to your life. I will try my best to convince you.

If there is a creation, there is a creator. When a creator creates something, there must be a purpose. Even if there is no purpose, there must be a reason for its existence. Sometimes, the reason could be deluding but not the value of the creation. Purpose, reason, and value may sound the same superficially, but they conceal a different and deep meaning underneath. For a lucid viewpoint, see the wheel; the purpose of the wheel is to facilitate transportation, the reason it was created is to move effortlessly by overcoming the friction between the ground and its surface, and the value of the wheel is unparalleled. A triangular, squared, or any other shape can't replace the shape of the wheel. Something could be created to solve contemporary problems, and something might be for imminent ones. So, time begins with the creation, and it always moves forward to meet the creator's goal to utilize his product. Thus, the final destination of everything is already devised, but the routes that connect from the beginning and the end are infinite. Like, the expiry date of medicine is already determined at its manufacture, the deadline for everything is fixed. Whether somebody fulfills its purpose by taking it to cure his illness or not, the medicine expires.

In this example, you think the intention wasn't fulfilled, but it's not true. Sometimes, the primary purpose itself has many side purposes. Again, going back to the example, the main goal of manufacturing the medicine could be earning. So, they didn't reach out to ills to reinforce taking medication. However, making money, providing jobs for the society, and so on was fulfilled, and then the medicine was expired. If the drug was manufactured with the sole purpose of curing diseases, it would definitely fulfill its goal, without any distractions, before its deadline. Some people may still argue. They said the sole purpose of a pen when it was created is to write, but what if it is only used to stab people until it becomes useless? According to them, this is a dilemma. Yes, it is. To understand this, we need to understand one more term- a facilitator, a person who can twist and turn the sole purpose or assist it in meeting the goal faster. In the example, the pen was created to fulfill the purpose of writing, but as soon as a bad-intentioned person held it, he imposed and enforced his own intention to stab people. Now, the pen has no choice but to follow the commands of the holder. This pen will never fulfill its creator's expectations. If the future is already determined during creation, how the heck on this earth did the pen not meet its destiny? There is a profound reason behind this. In this example, the level of consciousness of the creator and the user is the same; both are human. The creator can advise the user, but the user is entitled to make his own decision. Similarly, God created us in his own image, then we ate apples of wisdom which gave us more consciousness. After that, we turned and twisted the truth of everything as we liked. As a result, most of us are too busy fulfilling numerous side purposes and are completely oblivious of the only purpose we are created. When the user is as conscious as the creator, the user chooses to accept the purpose of the creation, but when the product is conscious by itself, there could be a revolution sooner or later because uncontrolled consciousness often drives enormous desires. When a creator creates something, the creation is bound to serve its purpose, but the product is conscious now. No matter how many times a creator tries to convince an axe about its sole purpose, if it is aware, it still wants to cut hair instead of the trunk of a tree. This is happening to mankind today.

If we time travel in the past and observe God creating a first human, will we be able to find our purpose? This is a silly, imaginative question. We won't be able to watch God creating us because the time, related to us, was originated only after the completion of our creation. So, theoretically, we can time travel only within a human time zone. We need to meet the beings within his time zone to know God's intention of creation, but we don't know both until today.

Humans have been seeking the answers for millenniums. In seeking, some accepted doctrines, which is religion, and some tried their own way and became more atheists. Those who relentlessly tried to prove the existence of God became religious, and those who did everything to disprove his existence became atheists. At the end of the day, both groups could not prove the truth. However, both did not stop speaking their mind on the matter; they were never sure. Forget them. You are yourself conscious; accumulate the facts and decide what you think. Be aware! Everything you do not know does not mean they don't exist. Whether you believe in creation or evolution, there is a flow of consciousness that is from simpler to complex. It is clear that something has started its journey towards its destination, but we do not know its destination. But the destination does not seem to be predetermined. If it was, then there would be no millions of species of living creatures. Or the consciousness was using the hit and trial method to reach our physical body level since we can assume that the human body is the best device for the consciousness to reside. But this thought process on evolution suggests that the level of consciousness that we have today and that of the chemical compounds of billion years ago is the same; only the device of the consciousness has been changed. There is no doubt that we are self-governing while talking about evolution from a compound to a human. This thought disagrees with the religious belief of God creating humans directly in human form, but the role of God in creating consciousness and putting it into chemical compounds cannot be denied, at least in this thought experiment.

No matter what we believe in, if everything around us can have many purposes in our lifetime, why can't you and I have one? Let's see how we can find the purpose of our life.

Knowing Oneself In-Depth

Almost every one of us thinks that we know ourselves from the depth in every aspect. In fact, we learn more about everything else than ourselves. When someone wants to know about us, we introduce ourselves with our name and some other essential information such as parent's name, the place where we from, age, race, and so on. If it is a job interview, we add information such as the skills that the company was looking for in a candidate. We discuss our hobbies and the things we like and dislike. We can explain everything we see in-depth and in detail. We can dissect things and see their mechanisms. This external world is easy to understand and examine with the help of tools, knowledge, and guidance, but while talking about knowing a person, it is almost an impossible process. I said it is impossible because of a few reasons. First, the perspective of a person to view the world keeps on changing based on the evidence and logic. Second, opinion on everything we have is based on the information we have accumulated so far. Third, the judgmental capacity we demonstrate is the outcome of our memory. If we examine people based on their knowledge about themselves, we will find most of them have become victims of the self-image they created. They unknowingly create an image according to the information they know and believe that they are that image. It is a powerful technique, but people have used it against their own progress. When we introduce ourselves, we babble the information we think right. But still, do we know ourselves? The average of our thoughts in an hour defines who we are, at least some part of us, with high accuracy. Desires are the seed of thoughts. The related information stored in our brain tries to get converted into thoughts to fulfill our desires. Thus, controlling over desires may help in reducing thought numbers. When there are a smaller number of thoughts managing our activities, we may see the world with a different point of view; a clairvoyant state of mind takes over. In this state of clarity, one can see himself in and out thoroughly. He will see all his weaknesses and strengths, good and evil, honest and crocked, lazy and intelligent side of himself. He understands that a chain is as strong as the weakest link of it. He will work on his weakness and moves forward. So, who you depend upon your surrounding that gives you strength or weakness? The average quality of your family, friends and the company you are with most of your time determines your quality. All these external things program you. As a result, you act like your father, friend, or someone who shaped your personality. Are you delighted introducing someone else in your place? Do not lose your identity, but before losing, find it first. Some processes I would suggest are as follows:

Noting Down All Your Capabilities

Write down on paper about the things you can do. It could be from cooking to programming. Note down even if you think it is useless for now. We are just making a long list of your ability. There is no doubt that we all have various skills and capabilities; we just do not notice them until it changes our life or until someone points out for us. Do not wait for sudden magic; the miracle has already happened, and that is you. Ask your friends if they see some unique ability to do something within you. Sometimes, we cannot see all aspects of our life, and we need someone to make us feel about it. We all have the brain that can learn anything we desired. Do not underestimate it. While writing the list, do not overthink. Just brainstorm about it, and when you are done with writing, delete the most unlikely ability that you think you do not have. Repeat the process until you have some adequate number in the list. We are focusing on your knowledge that can be positive or negative. If you are a brilliant pick pocketer, your pickpocketing ability is not a positive character. However, we cannot ignore your sleight of hand. While making a list, you are not judging good and evil. If you think some of your abilities are too negative in nature, think about converting them into positive ones before deleting them from the list and from your life. Creating a new habit or learning something new from scratch may take your time, effort, and energy. Also, there is no guarantee of success in the new one you just picked. Modify your strength as much as you can to convert it from evil to suitable if it is possible. If it is not, forget it. Making lists of this kind also helps us see the positive parts of our life. It provides us energy to overcome minor hindrances of life. You will feel good when you know you posse so many weapons in the form of your skills and ability to win the battle of life. As the list shrinks more and more in the deletion process, you reach closer and closer to meet yourself. You need to be honest with yourself in this process. Your conscious mind may want to trick you and make you chose the widely accepted character, which is not you. Delete those from the list. You're in the process of finding yourself, not defending the image you are living with. I am sure that the real you are far capable than the present one. The form of you in the present is the filter version of you; the conscious mind has filtered and stopped you from coming out. Just like a polarizer polarizes the light, the conscious mind polarizes our self-image. In the polarization of light, a polarizer does not let all elements of light pass through it. Before a beam passes through a polarizer, the electric and magnetic field vectors of the light wave travel in all directions vibrating in more than one plane, but as a polarizer comes on the way, it restricts the movement of those vectors to a single plane. As a result, the beam coming out of a polarizer is organized and vibrates in only one plane. I am just giving you an example to say how our mental state can block the full potential of us coming out of us. The impression we have regarding ourselves is nothing other than the recommendation of our conscious mind. The more the conscious mind is restless, the more we get relentless. To know the real you, you must tame the conscious level first. Making and editing the list of all qualities and abilities you have will make your conscious mind think that you are a genius and there is no risk from you to the sub-conscious level.

Phobias And Negativities

We all have something we hate to the death. At least, there has to be something you are scared of. Phobias and fears are the things that limit us and prevent us from experiencing life to the fullest. If you can, turn the fears into dares. If not, it's still passable; at least you know something about yourself. Make a list of things you are scared of to death. Note down all negativities and fears related to your phobias. My main suggestion is to overcome the fear. However, some phobias cannot be overcome through the conscious level of mind; it requires hypnosis to perform the job in many cases. If you cannot delete those phobias from your subconscious level, they become your limitation. Do not create a boundary to enclose yourself as much as possible. Look at the list you created and study those fears. Try to find out the reasons behind your fears. As you know the reasons, delete the respective phobias and face them. If it is about ferocious animals, ignore them because they are the common fears that we all have. The fear of height, fear of public speaking, fear of failing, and so on are the fears I am concerned about. If you have such, fight them and overcome them. As you go down in the list, making the number of fears lower, you boost confidence, and the chances of finding yourself are higher. The actual being of you never exists in negative vibration; to know yourself, you have to enhance your energy level. Otherwise, you will mistake something else for yourself.

Innate Skills

If we observe and analyze ourselves in deep, we may encounter some of the childhood skills that we still possess. Nature gives some strength and weakness to everyone. What is it? Ask yourself. Are you good at speaking and pursuing people? Are you physically strong? Can you run faster than anyone in the group? Can you influence people regardless of true or false information? Can you sing well? Ask all possible questions to yourself. If you find more than one quality in you, pick one to do best on it. Some people are logical by birth, and some are honest and truthful. Find something within you that separates you from the crowd. Even twin brothers and sisters have something uncommon and different in them. Do you have the ability to learn anything faster than anybody else in your friend circle? Are you the center of attraction of your friend group? There has to be something peculiar in your body, mind, or behavior that distinguishes you from anyone else. Actually, we all have our own unique personalities, but we get influenced by so many things that our character and skill get polluted. We never realize it and never work on polishing our own nature and innate talent. Instead, we carry on somebody else's personality as ours and try to live like others by imitation. As a result, we are neither somebody else nor ourselves.

Favourite Topics

Find out if there is something on which you can talk for hours without losing interest, and also, you can involve active listeners. Some people can talk about politics for hours. For me, I can talk about meditation and my mind forever without feeling tired. Suppose you were opening a YouTube channel on which topic or subject matter you would work on? How can you add your personality to it to make it unique? Some people have a soothing voice, and some have a clever mind. The topic you know more about could be your destiny. If you have some other favoring features for such activities, that could be the purpose of your life. Materialistic success and pleasure or popularity can be achieved even we are not made for it. However, one cannot sustain that position for long because he is not made for that specific reason. So, what is your favorite thing that you can do 20 hours a day and still feel energetic? There is something, but you still have not discovered it. Ask yourself every day until you find a satisfactory answer.

Focus On The Repeated One

If there is something you have been doing since childhood, as a hobby or interest, and you enjoy doing it, make it your purpose. You may not make your living out of it initially, but when you realize that it is your destiny and the purpose of your life, you will make something great out of it. No matter what field we pick, the struggle and the competition are inevitable. If you prefer something that you have been doing for a long and it is fun to you then, nothing else in the world can replace it. You just need to work harder this time because your hobby has become your purpose now. You should be able to add something new to it, something innovative. You cannot follow anyone; you are the leader. There have to be some ingredients you can put into the hobby to turn it into your identity. Though there are thousands of people in the same field, your point of view has to introduce a brand-new concept in the chosen area. This is the easiest one to find out within ourselves. Do you still paint? Do you still dance? Even if you do not do any of those that you used to enjoy when you were a kid, there has to be some habit or character you have been repeating over and again. You can make a list of them if you want. Tracking the purpose of life is not easy and not impossible either. There is no age limit to finding the meaning of life, but the sooner it is, the better because the struggle to fulfill one's purpose is a life-long process. Many people die without realizing their purposes. When they do not know their purpose, there is no chance of fulfilling it either. When the purpose is not fulfilled, something around us will be incomplete. We may not see the emptiness in the world physically, but we can notice the sound coming out of it; when you hit an empty vessel (metallic one), it produces a long ringing noise. The sound coming out of the world is not a relaxing one nowadays. A wrong person is sitting on the wrong seat; all over the world. Barely anyone knows their ability. Only a handful of people are contributing to the well-being of the world because they know that is their purpose. When we all find out our specific purpose, the earth's vibration will shift towards the better ones, and the atmosphere itself starts healing the wounds. When you find the meaning of your life, help others for the same. Spread the knowledge, spread the love.

Summary Of Chapter V

By default, humans as creatures have two purposes: 1st is living alive as long as possible, and 2nd is reproducing as many as possible to pass on the genetic information. If you are not mentally and spiritually awake, your life revolves around those two goals. You need to realize that there is more than just living and reproducing. Give yourself a direction and establish a reason for your existence. Whether you believe it or not, one of the essential purposes of human life is to lead others as well. If everyone realizes their ability, everyone will have a distinct character and knowledge. We all are different in some aspects, and we need to make it our strength. The thing you can do, no one else can justify it as good as you. I can accept that almost 90% of the population does not believe in the purpose of life. They keep on changing their minds on what they should do in their life. A group of people from 90% act like they live forever and waste their time without investing it into something fruitful. Some of them invest their entire time in indulging in luxuries. When someone from this group dies, only family, friends, and relatives cry for a few hours or days. But, when someone from the remaining 10% population dies, the entire world cries, and he would be remembered for centuries. We all have our unique capabilities to register our names in a 10% population list, but some are lazy. They are okay with sleeping tight; they do not wish to be awakened. They are okay in living under instructions from others because they cannot use their brains to be leaders. They might be thinking that saving ideas makes a person brainy, and using the brain more and more causes a decrement in brain size. As a result, people are acting dumb today. Do not fall in 90% of the population; find your purpose and see the world with a clear mind.

1. **Wake-up: 6 A.M.**
2. **Drink water, sip by sip.**
3. **Write dream tracking journal.**
4. **Drink the boiled water with my recipe.**
5. **Practice deep breathing in an open area.**
6. **Chant the mantra you created.**
7. **Physical exercise, flexibility, and Chess game**
8. **Practice visualization (does not have to be in the morning).**
9. **Be kind, and practice the willpower in as many activities as possible.**
10. **Eat healthy and detach yourself from unnecessary desires.**
11. **Establish a reason for your existence.**
12. **Chant the mantra you created before bed.**

CHAPTER VI

SETTING A HIGHER GOAL

"All who have accomplished great things have had a great aim, have fixed their gaze on a goal which was high, one which sometimes seemed impossible."- Orison Swett Marden

Get inside a car and have sit in the driving seat. Switch the gear to drive and press the gas. Merge to the highway and keep on driving. There must be a question in your mind right now; where am I going? Another experiment: Call a cab for a ride. When it arrives, tell the driver to keep on driving. Will the driver keep on driving? Let's imagine a ship that operates on GPS to travel from one place to another. You start the engine and push the ship forward but do not input the destination on GPS. What will happen to the ship? All the examples I gave above will have the same outcome: nothing good will happen at the end of the journey. Many people live without a destination, just like that ship left in the sea without its destination. In the beginning, there will be a lot of fun and excitement because everything is happening without a plan. Every day, there will be some uncertainty knocking at the door. You will love to have that unpredictable life which is called having a thrill. But how long can you sustain that thrill? How long can you ignore or combat uninvited and unwanted accidents? When you do not have a reason to fight against anything, you will not try hard. As a result, you get trounced. Those failures and mediocre experiences won't help you achieve anything great because you do not have any specific direction to use them. You will try every single thing to achieve success. In the process, you will lose a great deal of energy and time. When you start failing on one, you will find something else more appealing and safer. You keep on jumping from one idea to another. You can't stick with one because you do not know which stay longer in your life. You just chase things around. The closer you get to them, the further they approach. The struggle in such uncertainty is unbearable. Our life is a beautiful journey, and it should not be wasted in rambling around without any destination.

When we exactly know our destination, there will be no wastage of time finding the route, and there will be fewer chances of getting lost or getting into accidents. On the other hand, when we know our destination, and we plan on it, anything happens in the journey, we are prepared for it. When you are so clear about your destination, you do not need the assistance of anything to reach there. Each light posts, trees, rocks, and road tell you that you are getting closer to your goal. Imagine you are driving to your friend's house for the first time to attend a party. You have his address that you put into your GPS. You do not have to put your mind on roads anymore because GPS will surely take you to the destination. If you miss the exit, you will have to drive a little extra, but sooner or later, you will reach the destination. Suppose you take some time to find the house and then realize that you already know the place. Now, when you have to go back to your house from there, you do not need GPS. You already know every single light you have to cross. The map is in your mind. In this situation, even if you are slightly drunk, you can reach home quicker than the time it took you to get there. Similarly, if we know where we are going very well, the time for the journey can be managed. As a result, we will have plenty of time left for our family, friends, and relatives.

Nowadays, many of us are lost on the way, and many do not make it home in time. Their well-wishers are waiting to see them every moment. By saying 'on the way,' I mean living the life without control, and 'home' means the destination. From morning to evening, we work hard on something that we do not like. Every single minute we complain about the job we do, but we still have no choices besides continuing it. We repeat the same thing, do the same job every day, and expect something new as the outcome. Aren't we insane? Do you have dare to change your direction? Can you quit the job you hate? No. If you do so, how can you survive? This fear will never let you be free. Look, what you have received and what you have lost. The money you make in a month, 90% of which already know its destination to go. You are left with 10% of it, and its value is not so great either because it does not have a proper destination to go for its multiplication. You will plan a vacation, buy new stuff, and enjoy yourself with your friends and family. Now, you are left with none; You wasted your valuable time and traded it with things that would not give you last long pleasures.

From 9 A.M. to 5 P.M., you work like a donkey and wait the weekend to live your life. You chill Saturday, and from the morning of Sunday, you start whining. You will pass months and years like that. Have you ever talked to a dying person lying on the death bed? Whether he speaks or not, look outside through the window. How many people are gathering outside? When he dies, check his pocket if he has a checkbook, gold, or property with him. Did he take anything with him? If he could not take anything with him, what makes you so special that you think you can take whatever you want with you? If not, what is the reason behind 9 A.M. to 5 P.M.? While talking about the livelihood and the work you do not like, work like a dog, not like a donkey. I will tell you a story to make you understand the 'dog and donkey' phrase.

There was a poor washerman in a town. He had a dog and a donkey as pets. His job was to collect dirty clothes from the city, wash them and return them to make some money. Besides that, he used to cut down trees and sell them in the market for more income. For all purposes, he used to take his donkey with him to carry the load. From dawn to dusk, the donkey had to lift weights and worked harder. Every day when the washerman reached home, the dog used to come wagging his tail, jumping around him, barking and making happy noise, and licking his feet. Washerman would pat the dog with affection, and both would enter the house. The poor donkey who worked all day had to sleep outside, tolerating all bugs bits. On the other hand, the dog did not work hard like the donkey but still got to stay inside with the owner.

One day, the donkey decided to use its mind. In the morning, when the washerman was ready for his job, the donkey acted sick. Seeing it, energy less washerman decided to go to work without the donkey that day. The donkey felt good about his plan. In the evening, when the washerman arrived, the donkey jumped on him, wagging his tail, making a strange noise, and licking the washerman's feet. Washerman thought the donkey got crazy, and he started beating the donkey with a stick until it dropped down on the floor. The poor donkey was acting like a dog to get love from his owner. Instead, he got beaten up.

From this story, we need to observe two things; first, hard work barely pays off while talking about working for someone else, and second, imitation leads you to guilt. I would understand the second lesson of the story in a different way. If I were in the position of the donkey, working for others, I would never show my strength to the owner. Instead, I would use my mind and offer a different character that would be easier to do daily. You might know someone who does not know the job as much as you do and still gets paid as much as you in the same firm. If you act smart while working for others, you are that donkey lifting extra weights and wishing to get more love from the owner. Be smart, try to work less, and save more time for yourself, your family, and your friends. If you love your job and think that is your destiny, then go ahead; you will be happy no matter what. But, if your happiness is related to the company's goodwill, the paycheck, or the benefits they provide, you are living in an illusion; break it or be that donkey. This era is for smartness; I prefer smart work more.

Give a purpose to your life by setting a higher goal and see the magic it does. Most of the time, our higher goals protect us from committing anything crazy that could be detrimental. It provides us everlasting motivation. Every time you want to give up, we persist in your dream. Your goal will tell you about your weakness and help you find out ways to overcome the weakness. There is no doubt that the goal will set you apart from the crowd. Actually, goals are the fuel of life; the higher the goal, the better the life is.

When we talk about setting a goal, we talk about a famous technique known as SMART.

S = Specific
M = Measurable
A = Attainable
R = Relevant
T = Time – based

I would use this tool for smaller, short-term, day-to-day goals because the higher goal does not depend upon SMART. This goal is based on much minor and significant information about you. You can understand it as a long-term goal, but it has to be harder to achieve but not impossible. It may be different from that of your career but will motivate you throughout your life. Be specific and set the goal based on your interest, character, and capacity. When you know yourself and realize the uniqueness of your personality, you will achieve something different from anybody else. It does not need to be measurable, attainable, relevant, or time-based for now. Set an ideal dream as the goal, and work for it. You do not have to tell anyone about your plan, but remind yourself every minute. It's mental work at large.

When the same information and process is repeatedly going on in your mind, a subconscious mind has chances to interact with your thoughts. If it is so, you will find ways to fulfill your desires or meet your goal. I have heard many stories of people whose last wish is to see their son or grandson before his death, and as soon as the dream is fulfilled, the person dies. In other words, I have experienced the power of setting a higher goal a few times that save my life and keep me away from committing evil deeds and crimes. These goals circulate self-control in our minds that restrict us from any evil thoughts and deeds we may end up doing. When you do the visualization, practice a lot with your goal, and become your invisible guide. As a result, you know what is good and bad for it. You might have seen some people going to bed early and waking up early. If you ask them for a reason. They may not be able to answer what is going on in their minds and motivate them to do so.

Even if they try to explain how they respond to a command of their mind, you would not understand. Therefore, you may hear, "It became my habit" from them as the answer. To make a habit of waking up early is not that easy unless there is a solid compulsive reason or motivation. If such a difficult discipline becomes your habit, healthily, not because of insomnia, nothing can stop you from achieving greatness. But is it possible to establish a pattern without setting any goal? On the other hand, simply writing a list of goals and never thinking about them after it will never do anything to your life. It is right that everything starts from thoughts, but if you limit the ideas and goals into thoughts only, then nothing will happen. Do something every day related to your dream so that you get closer to your goal gradually. A positive and higher purpose is like a best friend that is always with you. By contacting it, you will do so many positive works that people will appreciate your presence wherever you go. When you fail to do something great, you already achieve success. You ought to be relentless. You will see the friends around you; they are different from those around you. While you did not have any higher goals, your company will change. The entire universe will help you to get you to your destination.

We talked about the importance of setting a higher goal, but are there any chances of achieving it? First of all, when the goal is high enough, and a person is persistent towards it, the chances of living an ideal life are always high. There is no chance to be a complete failure because the goal is still so far from you, and it may take a lifetime to achieve it, but you never give up. For example, winning a noble prize for a physicist is a high goal, and a person can follow the SMART technique. If he works hard for ten to fifteen years, the goal is achievable. But, if the same person sets up a dream that he wants to educate every town and countryside of the world, this is a significantly higher goal. We can see plenty of obstacles and issues that can come across on his path. He will have to sacrifice his own family life for others. The goal is so high that he would not be able to complete it in his lifetime, but the most undeniable fact is that achieving some fractions of his goal is far better and more humane than ten or twenty of our fully completed goals.

There is a secret method to set up a higher goal based on the universal law of attraction principle. When I say the law of attraction, many people have questions if the law of attraction works. You have heard it and tried it; based on your experience, you do not have evidence to support if it works. You are right, but that is limited in your case only. In my case, it has worked. Before we understand how the universal law of attraction works, we need to know more about the universe and how it works in terms of energy.

As we discussed in chapter I, we already realized that everything we see is energy and vibration. We also philosophically, logically, religiously, and scientifically proved that everything around us is conscious to some extent. In that sense, the entire universe is a substantially aware body, and all animate and inanimate things are constantly thinking; in other words, they are releasing waves. We believe that to be able to, they need to have a brain, but we are not talking about the brain; we discuss the mind and waves. The brain is a device that allows the mind to make plans. But the thought in the waveform is released out of everything and is almost everywhere. Gold, diamond, money, wealth, and all matters are vibrating in a specific frequency related to them. As humans, we are provided with the most advanced device to capture such frequency and vice versa, and that is our brain. There is a way to attract such frequency towards us. To understand that phenomenon, let us see how a radio catches signals because this is precisely the same way we can catch the frequency we want. We are getting deeper and deeper in this thought process. I have not entirely abandoned the previous topic that we were discussing, the universal law of gravitation. We will come to that point later, but at this moment, let's see how a radio works.

We need an antenna to pick the radio waves out of the air. The antenna helps to increase the number of radio waves to go to the transmitter. Since thousands of radio signals present in the air, an antenna will collect all of them. It does not have any sense of selection. To separate unwanted waves, the radio receiver needs a tuner. A tuner is basically a device that works with the principle of resonance. Tuner resonates with a particular frequency and rejects or ignores all the other unnecessary signals or waves in the air. The function of the tuner is to pass only one frequency through it. The detector, next, extracts DJ's voice out of that one wave. This detector is made up of a diode that allows current to flow through in one direction but not into the other. Finally, the signal is amplified by using transistors to send it to the speaker. So, the flow of frequency through different parts of the device looks like this:

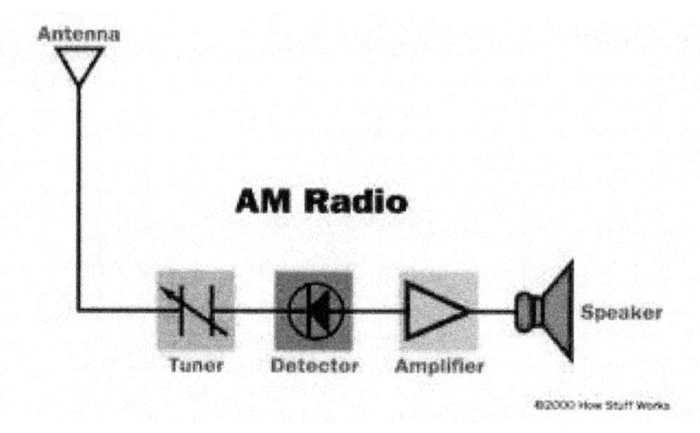

Figure 1 Diagram is created by How Stuff Works.

In this diagram, we see that the frequency collected by the antenna has converted into sound. Let's compare our physical body with the radio. Different sense organs help our brain absorb various frequencies in the air; they work as antennas. The conscious mind rejects a lot of frequencies from reaching them to the sub-conscious level. Thus, the conscious mind works as a tuner and the sub-conscious as the detector. The superconscious mind acts as an amplifier, but most of us rarely excess it. Our entire body performs as a speaker but does not take the word speaker literally.

In this analogy, the radio converts selected frequency into sound, and our brain converts the entire body into the attractor, just like a magnet, of a chosen frequency. As a result, a person vibrates with the frequency of the things he desired, and those things come towards him because of his attraction power. As far as I know, there is no research regarding the hypothesis I put above, but I have seen the effects of the universal law of attraction in my own life. We understood how the frequency work, but how to pick the right frequency? This question may arise in your mind too. There is no scientific device created yet to download the frequency of gold and diamond into our minds. Yes, we have binaural beats, but is that the actual frequency of the things we desire? However, the conscious mind has to be tuned, or the frequency won't do anything. All the efforts I am making here in this book are to convince your conscious mind so that you will be its master. To absorb the frequency well, you need to be around with such frequencies as much as you can. For example, you want to be a millionaire, you need to vibrate with the frequency of wealth and prosperity. If you are poor, you need to work on changing the vibration before starting a considerable investment. To change your vibration, try to have some money in your wallet all the time, wear some gold, if possible, be around rich people. You do not have to accept the 'fake it, until you make it' principle because while performing this fake demonstration, your conscious mind knows it, and you cannot convince it that you are not faking. Then, you will never get what you want. Just work with the sources you have; you need the frequency, and it does not matter the quantity at this point in time.

Now, coming back to the universal consciousness, the entire universe is conscious, and everything is interrelated. When something happens to one, the other gets affected as well. Each and everything we see in the universe is the manifestation of all combined thoughts, the waves of all animate and inanimate matters. Thoughts of one can harm others too. One's thought is a tiny microscopic part of cosmic thought.

Nevertheless, it has the energy to create turbulence in the universe if it is amplified with a superconscious mind. When you become a magnet of a particular frequency, the universe itself opens the doors for your success. As a result, many people cannot see the opportunity but you. You do not have to work harder to achieve success as much as other less-tuned individuals. You will be vibrating harmoniously with the universe.

I have seen a lot of people living this principle unknowingly. I have a few friends who get the best out of anything they do; no consecutive failures because they are resonant with the pleasant vibration of the universe. There is no such thing as luck, but the law of vibration works amazingly for some people, making us believe they are so lucky. When the majority of the cosmic thoughts start working for you, the manifestation of anything is possible.

The Right Way To Set A Higher Goal

After studying numerous biographies of successful people and almost all major religious holy books, I think the hint is that we should involve others in it when we set up a goal. I mean, our goal should be beneficial for more people. When I set up a goal that is for the welfare of my family and me only, then I will have to put an enormous effort to achieve success. In this case, my consciousness is working in favor of me. Maybe my family's consciousness is also helping me to create the power of manifestation. But this goal is filled with selfishness. Another huge part of cosmic consciousness finds it worthless to help me. When we are conscious, I am talking about the conscious mind; we are self-centered because the conscious mind's job is to take care of ourselves first to stay alive. If the universe is composed of all conscious matters, then all matters are concerned for their existence; existing is their first priority. The level of consciousness in the inanimate matter is ignorable, but the cosmic consciousness is composed of the upper, lower, and all kinds of consciousness. All those minds work for mutual benefits.

On January 1st, 2011, a research journal was published by Simone de La Tour and Kevin de La Tour on 'Original mind and cosmic consciousness in the co-creative process.' They concluded their research in their word as "It is necessary to become more disciplined in our efforts of operating from the original mind. This allows us to more actively participate—in greater alignment—with the cosmos as a partner in the creative process." Original mind refers to the level of mind that involves intuition, illumination, self-conscience reaching toward the inner self (Tour et al.,2011). The research paper's authors show that a harmonious relationship of an individual's mind with cosmic consciousness is necessary for any creative process. We can't ignore the universe and simply be selfish. If we only try to benefit ourselves, then there is a real struggle. Let's take an example and try to understand this point of view. Suppose you live in the poor countryside where there is no proper road. You decide to connect your backyard to the road for your comforts and business. You will have to do everything by yourself or hire people to get the job done. Your goal of extending your backyard or connecting it with the road does not include others neighborhoods beneficial. Some good things might happen, such as job opportunities for some people for a few days, but the main intention is not providing a job or doing something for the welfare of others. Thus, no one wants to put effort there. On the contrary, if you plan to work for the welfare of the entire neighborhood that includes your goal, you may get assistance from everyone. For example, if you find a way to construct a better road connecting your neighborhood and town that passes by your back yard, then you will benefit more. When you set up your goal, wrap your goal with a mutual goal so that everyone will work harder to make your dream true. As a materialistic person, what do you desire? Wealth, health, popularity, and peace of mind, isn't it? It is a rare combination but not impossible to have all of them being together.

I studied the life of many Rishis or gurus from ancient Sanatan dharma. I have found that all gurus were richer than the king of the nation. When the king lost everything in the war, he used to go to the Ashramas of Rishis to borrow some wealth to protect the nation. Those Rishis were popular, wealthy, healthy, and always in ecstasy mood. Their family life was outstanding; they did not quit the material world. They were prosperous from all aspects of life, in and out. They were spiritual teachers. We need to understand that they never set up a goal to be a millionaire for themselves. In fact, they never set a goal to be wealthy. Earning wealth is the outcome of their magnificent goal; to enlighten the world with knowledge, empathy, and positivity. They decided to help millions, and the cosmic mind helped them from all aspects. If you are bringing happiness to many, those people will definitely bring everything you want. It's like there are hundreds of issues at your work, and you are the only one out of thousands of employees who can fix it. Imagine how the company will treat you; they will provide you much more than you had anticipated. When you target a huge population of humans or animals or plants or everything for their benefits at large, you are the leader. All group members will work to please you because no one else thinks about them again if you drop the idea. The leader has to survive. In the war, the same thing happens; when a party leader is dead, the war is over. Soldiers gave their lives to protect their leader from saving the mission. When a lot of people are associated with your goal, success is inevitable. Such association may be direct or indirect. While saying indirect, I mean the association you will create through the cosmic mind or cosmic consciousness. You do not have to believe in this, but the cosmic mind will still work for you. If you want to make more money to donate more, this thought may manifest quicker. But who wants to work for others? When you set a goal, you are the one who has to work for it. No magical gin will appear to carry out your plans, but the level of struggle and the amount of pleasure you can receive definitely gets high. When the universe wants to offer you success, many coincident occur, everything will be done at the right time, everyone will be happy with you, and you become the center of attraction in the crowd.

If you want the universe to continuously work in your favor, you must go by its rules. You must involve the bigger part of the universe in your goal. The goal has to be auspicious for everyone and everything as much as possible. This is only a theory I came up with after studying the biography of many popular political leaders, spiritual leaders, and scientists. There was something common in all successful people, and it was setting a higher goal that involved the benefits and welfare of many people. I personally experienced the difference before and after setting a higher goal. Now, I am more disciplined, tolerant, patient, persistent, and confident. I would not say that you would be a noble person after setting a higher goal. A goal can be positive or negative. Adolf Hitler had his own higher goal that made him an evil person in history. He did well for some and evil for more people. However, the people who were included in his goal supported him, and still, some people admire him. I do not judge right or wrong. It's you who have to decide what to aim for, and now you know the secret of the universe.

After You Decide On Your Goal, You Need To Register It In Your Mind

When you set up your goal so high and unrealistic that it does not match your character, knowledge, and experience, then the chances of a conscious mind rejecting it are high. You need to find a loophole to override the conscious mind and reach the subconscious level in such a case. Or follow the highway; convince the conscious mind about your goal. If you are practicing my instructions from the beginning, you know the process to convince your conscious mind. In this chapter, I will discuss a technique that can be done at any time, but bedtime, right before you fall asleep, is ideal. My primary goal is to make you ready for the spiritual journey, and I am taking you one step closer to it through every chapter. The technique I am going to explain is my favorite one. Many of my students have benefited from it, and I have experienced it on myself too. This technique is prevalent, and usually, it is done to relax the mind and body. Its procedures at bedtime are as follows:

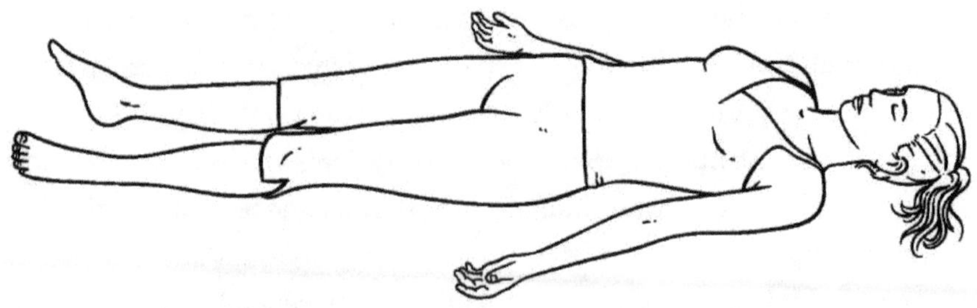

Fig.: Savasana Pose

1. While lying on the bed, face the ceiling and spread your arms and legs straight. You can do wisdom mudra (Gyan mudra) of hand if you want. It is bringing index finger and thumb together and pressing each other slightly.

2. Bring your focus on everything in the bed and room that can cause discomfort and irritate you in a minute. If you know some, fix them right away and refocus to find more. You need

to close your eyes while doing this.

3. When there is no discomfort at all, bring your attention towards the center of the eyebrows with closed eyes. Try to hold the attention for a few seconds there. When thoughts start arising, bring your focus towards the breath. Do not control your breath or thought; just observe them. Feel the sensation of breathing through the nose to the lungs. Now, slowly move your attention towards your feet.

4. Visualize both your feet's toes and try to feel the sensations happening there. Senses such as coolness, rubbing of the blanket, the touch of bedsheets, and so on. Try to feel if there is some pain or discomfort in the feet. If you feel pain, imagine that the pain is releasing from your feet in the form of a wave. Suggest to yourself that your toes and feet are getting lighter and lighter.

5. Move towards calves and shins and repeat the same process that you just did for feet and toes.

6. Continue the process. Take your time and feel every part of your body, including the intestine, liver, heart, kidney, and blood circulation. Do this process until you feel drowsy. At some point, your conscious mind gives up, and you feel sleepy. This self-induction into the hypnotic state you have created is called self-hypnosis. During this phase, the conscious mind is inactive or so tired. It will not be able to stop our thought from reaching the subconscious level. You may fall asleep, but you have to make sure that you tell your wish in 3 words before falling asleep. This is the golden period of being conscious and subconscious at the same time.

This can be practiced during the daytime as well, but you need to make sure that no one will disturb you while performing it. Practice this every day for your higher goal. Once it is registered in your subconscious level, related and required things come towards you automatically to fulfill your dream. You can cure yourself of several afflictions. Some people have claimed that they cure themselves of illness by using this technique and healing others. Anyway, the effectiveness of self-hypnosis to ourselves is unparalleled. An academic journal published on September 1st, 2019, on 'Clinical applications of self-hypnosis' by Adam D. Eason and Benjamin A. Parris confirms the effectiveness of self-hypnosis. In this research paper, people applied self-hypnosis in various situations, such as pain, pregnancy labor, stress, anxiety, and hypertension. Researchers reviewed 22 other studies to confirm the outcome. They found 18 research out of 22 ensuring the effectiveness of self-hypnosis, and thus, they concluded in their journal from the reviewed research that self-hypnosis is effective (Eason et al.,2019). When you practice the above exercise every day, you will find your own way to visualize your body and healing it on your own. This entire process can take you an hour since you are a beginner. Once you practice regularly, you will learn to scan your body within a minute or in a few seconds one day. This is a particular technique I do to re-energize myself when I am too tired but has to go on. I personally take 6 to 15 seconds to scan my entire body and refill enthusiasm within me. I used to do this while running to complete the race. If you can apply self-hypnosis, 10 min of such hypnotic sleep would refresh you as much as you get after 4 hours of sleep. On March 5th, 2021, when I was driving from California to Texas, I went for 20 and half hours straight without rest, break, food or sleep. I used this technique, and in 48 hours, I slept only 4 hours due to some critical reasons. I am just trying to show you that it is achievable.

Summary Of Chapter VI

Setting a goal is not a magical process that turns thoughts into reality, but it will definitely open your mind to see the ways and opportunities more than ever before. Whether short-term or long-term and larger or smaller, setting goals always motivates us to work harder for the desired outcome. If it is the short-term one, we feel like we achieved everything in our life after accomplishing it. As a result, we may tend to become less progressive. On the contrary, if we aim for something great that is beneficial for many people or animals or anything, the chances of accomplishing our goal are high. Our goal always gets connected with us in our mind in any situation of life and constantly motivates us to stay on the right track and prevent us from doing something terrible. It is impossible to have mentors walking around with us all the time, but our goal is to tell us what should be done and what should be avoided in life. It teaches us to be disciplined. It connects us with more people. We constantly become optimistic and progressive. After knowing the secret of goal setting strategy, you will start thinking about the welfare of more people. When more people are associated with your task, achieving any goal is more straightforward than trying alone.

Also, the result we get from including more people in our goal will be amplified. We also discussed how the cosmic consciousness acts as our friend when we are disciplined and focus on the welfare of everyone. Trust in yourself first, and then trust the universe; the thing you have desired is on the way for its delivery. As Matthew 7:7 from the bible says, "Ask, and it will be given to you; seek, and you will find; knock, and the door will be opened to you." This is the time for realization and setting a higher goal, and tomorrow is the time to receive it and enjoy the success. If you practice all the exercises I mentioned in this book, I am optimistic that sooner or later, you will experience what I actually mean. From today onwards, your daily routine should look like this:

1. **Wake-up: 6 A.M.**
2. **Drink water, sip by sip.**
3. **Write dream tracking journal.**
4. **Drink the boiled water with my recipe.**
5. **Practice deep breathing in an open area.**
6. **Chant the mantra you created.**
7. **Physical exercise, flexibility, and Chess game**
8. **Practice visualization (does not have to be in the morning).**
9. **Be kind, and practice the willpower in as many activities as possible.**
10. **Eat healthy and detach yourself from unnecessary desires.**
11. **Exercises to find the reason of your existence.**
12. **Self-hypnosis before bed/anytime.**
13. **Chant the mantra you created before bed.**

CHAPTER VII

THE WEALTH

"Only buy something that you'd be perfectly happy to hold if the market shuts down for ten years."- Warren Buffett

There was a wealthy merchant in some city. He had a huge business of diamonds. He was making a well-off life with the import and export business of jewelry. He had a good name in the town. He was blessed with a beautiful wife and a son. Everything a man desires, he had made possible in his life for his family. He was not born rich, though, but his son was born with a silver spoon in his mouth. As the son grew teenager, the man wanted him to get involved in his diamond business, but the son did not show any interest. The man tried several times to bring him into the business, but there was no avail. The man thought that his son was taking everything, wealth, business, and property, for granted. Thus, one day, he decided to take his son to a poor slum area several miles away from the city. Man wanted his son to see how it feels to live a poor life. Maybe after this visit, he would be motivated to learn the business and start earning from the teenage, the man thought. They left for the village. After a few hours, they reached a poor slum area with no tall and new buildings. The houses were old and shabby; some of them did not have walls and ceilings. Cattles and pets were roaming around. There was a huge river nearby. People were busy in their daily business; some were working in the field, and some were weaving mats. Children were playing on the ground. They kept walking through the slum to observe the lifestyle of people

from close. There was a different aroma in the village. They could hear the beautiful sounds of birds and could feel the fresh air. The son had never been to places like that before. Dirt roads, potholes everywhere, and mud had made their shoes dirty. In the evening, after seeing and experiencing the poor life from close, they returned home.

While coming back, the father asked his son, "How was the trip?"

"It was okay." The boy sighed.

Noticing less enthusiasm in the boy's voice, the man thought that the boy might have understood the hardship of poor people. He asked the boy with inner joy, "Now, you know how poor lives, don't you?"

"I already knew how poor lives, but today I saw the reality that how rich lives." The boy looked into the eyes of his father and spoke sarcastically.

"What do you mean? I did not get that. Can you tell me what you learned from the trip without beating around the bush?" The annoyed man lost his patience.

The boy looked at his father with wet eyes and said, "The house we live in definitely has fans and AC, but people living in the village have a blast of natural fresh air. We have a lavish 20 feet wide swimming pool in our backyard; they have an endless river. Our ceiling and walls are painted with bright, beautiful colors and paintings, natural beauty like tress and real stars. We have a fence around our house to protect us; they do not need it because they protect each other. We have a small yard, and they have infinite land up to the horizon. We have a dog; they have plenty of them. We are bounded by rules of money and wealth, but they are free and happy. We have more money and fewer people around us. I was living this poor life for a long and today, you showed me the life of the rich. Thank you, dad, for today's experience." He hugged his father tight. His voice was shaking and depicting as if he had realized the truth.

The father could not say anything. He got water in his eyes. All of his life, he worked hard to earn money to become wealthy and happy. Now, it was becoming meaningless to him. He realized that wealth is just a barrier between humans and his happiness. People need to be pleased with what they have; wealth definitely cannot buy you happiness. The more money, the eviler you will be. Learn to be happy at any cost because, at the end of the day, your satisfaction counts more than anything else in this world, and money cannot buy you everything. So, think about it! Hold onto your 'everything' and do not run after something that cannot give you anything. We are here to enjoy; let's enjoy life. We are here for mankind. Serve all with open hearts and share happiness. Don't waste your valuable time and energy in chasing the evil; the money."

This is a story I heard from somewhere. There is a significant meaning of life in this story. It shows us the reality of our lives where many of us are chasing immediate happiness, which is not permanent. We live for things such as money that make us slaves and keep us away from our people; we need to wake up and break the chain of unhappiness tying us from being free. Isn't it?

BULLSHIT! BULLSHIT!! SOME MORE BULLSHIT!!!

I am still looking for the person who told me the story because I immensely dislike the connotation of the story. Before explaining my personal opinion on why I hate this story, let's analyze the story from reality. The boy said the poor people have a blast of fresh air, beauty of never-ending river, vast area of land stretching all the way up to the horizon, and neighbors helping each other. The story is so lame that it looks like someone who is well off has written this story because there is no truth. Have you ever imagined how many people die of heat and cold every year? The fresh air that the character of the story is mentioning does not last even all day. The wall and the ceiling of the shabby house do not keep people safe from rain and storm. The most beautiful river can become a reason for the death of countless poor people because they simply cannot afford a water filter. The story overlaps the heart-wrenching cries of

hungry children with the pleasant songs of birds. Just by visiting the place for a couple of hours, the boy realized that the rich lived a misfortune life and vice-versa. So ridiculous. The story helps to prove that the grass on the other side is always green, but nothing else.

There is also chaos, social evils, crimes, and diseases if there is an extreme poverty level. As the boy mentioned in the story, the feeling of co-operation and guarding each other is possible only when there is money flow in people adequately. The storyteller seems to be confused with the term middle class family and the poor. He misunderstood the middle-class family as the poor; he could belong to the middle-class. I will tell you the reality of what poor refers to.

The poorness is that when you have to go to bed with an empty stomach, and it is your second night in a row, you haven't eaten a single grain for two days, and you are just a child. You afford only the low quality of food, and you have to separate bugs from the beans and rice after it is cooked, and it worsens if you are a vegetarian. The heart breaks when your mother goes to do labor all day and brings you food that she was supposed to eat in her lunch because you have not eaten anything all day. It is painful to know that your teenaged child gets bullied because he goes to school in a shabby uniform with two holes on the back of his pants. There is a severe issue when you introduce yourself as a middle-class person when all of your middle-class friends live a different standard of life.

The main issue now I can see in society is wrong people are explaining false experiences without experiencing them on their own. I remember an incident related to this fact. It was in my childhood there was a poem competition in the town. I knew a person who participated in the competition. He recited his composition about a poor orphan who helps others and does not accept money in return. The conclusion of the poem was money cannot replace the serving hand and caring heart. Everyone loved it; I overjoyed too. He won 2nd place; he deserved it.

While writing this chapter, I went back to the time, mentally, and re-visualized his reciting. He came from a millionaire background. He was the only son of his family, and they owned many lands throughout the country. He was the one who used to carry 50 bucks as pocket money every day in childhood. He was explaining what hunger is, what scarcity is and what adversity is. The fun part was, the advice he was giving us to carry home was serving hands is more important than money and wealth. Of course, he could say that because he was very used to having servants at home. Another incident I remember when I was studying at Idaho State University in 2012. I used to be a personal tutor for students from Arab. He said that his bank took $25k out of his account and did not understand where the money went. He lamented because his father sent him money for the entire year, and $25k was disappeared. He showed me the receipt. I had to look at it several times because I could not believe it; his father transferred $500k into his account, and that was for one academic year. Since I was spiritual and money did not mean anything to me, I would pass out there otherwise. One day, he invited me to join the feast in the evening. He said the day before was his last day of fasting. I got interested to know more about it. Ramadan was just done, and he had fasted for a whole month. I asked him if there were reasons and history behind it. He opened my eyes with so much good information. One of his points was fascinating to me. He said fasting reminds him how it feels to be hungry, poor, and less fortunate. I realized that there are so many good people in the world. He also said a person has to be wealthy by heart; money comes and goes. He also showed less concern for money. I was happy that so many people have similar thoughts about money. Today, when I think about both incidents, I understand that many of us are brainwashed about the meaning of money. Rich people are actually spreading rumors about money. When my friend fasted for a long time, he tried to understand the hunger of a starving person by imitation, but the actual adversity does not stop there. A poor person has to struggle every moment for everything differently, and living in such pain is unbearable. These misfortunate people also firmly believe that money is an evil thing.

I have a similar song of my life. People preached to me to be happy all the time, I obeyed them. I tried to dissect things to find happiness. I separated bugs from the bean and made it edible, which gave me happiness. I wore old and torn clothes for years, and I was still happy. Many of my minor childhood desires were never fulfilled; I never complained because I was told to be happy. I always hunted the positive things of my life to find a reason to be happy. In reality, I had two choices to be happy; 1st, drugs, and 2nd, the moral principles of books I read. I chose the second; believing in bookish knowledge and the principles set up by failures. Later, I rejected both and started my own way of happiness. I realized that being poor and being happy simultaneously is as hard as chewing the iron rod. I made myself capable of earning as much money as I want, but my spiritual teachers and gurus suggested me make only enough that is required to survive; I followed them respectfully. I was told that money is the source of illusion and lust that invites troubles and evils only. I remember an evil incident that happened because of money in my neighborhood. Three elder brothers killed the youngest one for the shake of wealth going to him as heritage. Actually, they killed him a month ago, cut him into smaller pieces, and dumped the body into a ditch. When it started stinking, people discovered the dead body, which was totally decayed and hard to identify. I was a kid; however, I observed every single piece carefully. Now, people stamped the fact that wealth is evil. Whenever people talked about wealth, they started using the incident to show how money can motivate you to kill your own people. After seeing such an unforgettable incident, plus hearing everyone confirming the evil character of money, my relationship with it became more appalling. I started making just the right amount of money and donated a large amount. I thought I was achieving greatness and would get all happiness in life.

In 2018, a life-changing incident happened in my life that burst the bubble in which I was enclosed. I analyzed what wrong was with me. I found the weakest part of my life, and it was the wealth; I was making more than enough money, but still, nothing was saved or invested. Money was just coming and going. I fulfilled my parents' desires, but my personal bank account was always less than $500. I was getting out of the US army in 5 months, but I suddenly added a short-term goal to my list. It decided to see $100,000 worth of cash before December 2019. My company was deploying to the Middle East in 4 months for the second time. It was a great opportunity for me to make the targeted amount. I tried to extend the contract for the deployment, but the battalion said I cannot just extend it, I had to sign another contract which would make me stay in the army for longer, and my other goals would be affected. My doctor from medical did not allow me to deploy because I was taking some medicine that may not be available in the Middle East. But I did not lose my heart and still thought about meeting my goal in time. I followed the exact method that I described in this book for setting goals and empowering willpower. After two months, I got a call from the battalion, and they said that they changed the rule just for me. I could extend it for as long as I want. After a few days, the doctor also gave me the approval, and I got the opportunity to take part in the second tour. I got involved in so many monetary transactions in that deployment. I lent money to others that offered me a small amount of interest every month, and I invested in stocks and cryptocurrency. Luckily, I made money on almost everything I invested. At the end of 2019, I exceeded my goal with $3,029 after sending money to my parents every month. My goal had certainly shown me the way. All the stocks I picked in 2019 have done so well today. For example: I bought 2000 of chain link @ $0.43/each and sold 1000 of them @ $8 and 1000 at @ $50. Doge coins = bought 100,000 of them @0.0019. The total investment was $190. Sold 50,000 of them in May 2021, made almost $20,000, and still owned half of it. Riot = bought @ $1.87 and sold at $60, it hit higher than $60 later, rite aid = bought at $6.7 and sold at $25, XRP = bought at 0.16, 23,000 of them, still holding it. Tesla = this is the biggest blunder I made = waited for the price of $35 to buy 850 of them = reached $37 = missed opportunity. I did not invest in it because my goal was to make 100k by making day trade with the largest amount available. I was also using margin that compelled me to perform day trade. There are other stocks I picked for friends, and they skyrocketed too.

The experience I am sharing here is not to show you how good I am at trading; no matter how good are you, the market will smash you if you do not get out at the right time. Actually, I am not good at all; I just use my intuition, and I received what I asked for. Imagine if I had tesla at $35 and sold at $860 in Jan 2021. I would have almost 730k, theoretically. I did not ask for it while setting my goal, and I did not receive it either. I am not mentioning my stocks picks to brag about my knowledge. In reality, I am trying to show you that everyone can transform their inner vibration to become a magnet of wealth. I finished my time in service and got out in 2020 with the cash I desired. I will share how I managed to change the negative vibration I had about money sometime later.

I never want to continue something in my life with many doubts. When I was thinking about getting involved in the materialistic world as much as in the spiritual world, I was scared of getting lost in the fake world. I knew I could not get a proper answer from any spiritual gurus. Thus, I decided to search for the truth by myself. 'VEDAS,' the oldest spiritual book conformed by science with carbon dating, was my first choice. Rig Veda Samhita vi-71-6 clearly mentions that one shall produce wealth for the present and future and eradicate poverty. The term 'wealth' appears several times in Vedas. Quran allows us to be wealthy, and Bible wants us to ask so that it will be given. I found that money is not evil at all, as people were mentioning. I grew up hearing a proverb that Devi Saraswati (goddess of wisdom and arts) and Devi Laxmi (goddess of wealth) do not stay together. That means if you are wise, you die poor. My idol Nikola Tesla was intelligent, and he died in poverty. Sir Isaac Newton, the most outstanding scientist ever born, lost his wealth in stocks. That made me believe the proverb without questioning it for so many years. These kinds of proverbs and sayings are famous for poor people; the rich do not find it worthwhile to accept it as the truth.

If somebody wants to eradicate poverty, they need to focus on the mindset of the poor. Instead of feeding the fish, the poor need to be taught fishing. There is a lot of negativities in the mind of the poor regarding wealth. They struggle day and night to make barely enough to survive. Still, the hate towards the wealthy and wealth is prominent in them. Money has to be your slave; you should never accumulate wealth through wrong deeds, or you will definitely face a bitter consequence. Treat the money like you treat your girlfriend; a mental game: You need to establish a deep relationship with money first. Imagine the money as a beautiful woman (or man) you will fall in love with. You must treat money how you like to treat your girlfriend. If you have a real human girlfriend, try to mistreat and hate her, ignore her, and tell her that she is less important than your family and friends. The moment you speak the truth, the relationship is over. You may see her around if you live in the same town, and you may talk to her now and then, but the mirror has already broken; it is hard for you to get her back in your life. Similarly, if you keep on hating money, your relationship with it will be embittered. You may have money coming and leaving you, but she will never stay with you because you do not take care of her. I hope you do not take my words so literally and marry the hundred-dollar bill. My point is, do not use the money for stupid reasons such as drinking, smoking, and unnecessary shopping. Use her for needs but not for all wants. Make her feel that how much you like her and love her. I am just comparing two different kinds of stuff, but both behave in the same way. Money needs plenty of your attention. When you do not care about her, she goes away. Her nature is similar to humans; you cannot lock her up forever. If you do not love her, she will find someone who cares for her. She has many choices. If you resonate with her frequency, a deep relationship is established. After that, she will never leave you. Everything you touch will be priceless. My words and sentences in this paragraph sound like poetry, but it's the rule of money I just told you. Treat the money how you like to be treated. Approach her in the right way, impress her with your virtuous acts, and attract her with your acts of kindness.

Loving the money and chasing it are two different things. When you intensely admire someone, you do not chase her; instead, you set her free. The more freedom you give to your loved ones, the more they come towards you with their will. If you decide to hide your girlfriend, enclosing her in the locker, she won't love you back. Similarly, take a hundred-dollar bill and make a tight fist to secure it; you may lose the opportunity to collect more money because your hand is not open for more. When the fist is loose, the money is free. A freely circulated cash will generate more of it eventually; things go around, come around.

After establishing my relationship with money, I decided to read self-help books regarding cash. I bought a kindle and downloaded 150 best-selling books. I took my kindle with me in 9 months of army tour in 2019. I challenged myself by implementing 'one book a day' reading exercises. To meet my challenge, I used to wake up at 0350 every day. My peers, juniors, and leaders thought that I would quit it soon, I continued for the entire deployment. I read 133 books in 6 months on investment, business, writing, blogging, programming, and passive income sources. I used the super-learning technique to read that many books in little time that I had. It's a method that trains your mind to grasp only the summary of books or chapters. I finished reading books such as the richest man in Babylon, rich dad poor dad, the intelligent investors, think and grow rich, the 10 X rule, the art of the deal, why we want you to be rich, millionaire mindset, the millionaire next door, and so on. So many studies and hard work helped me become the magnet of money for that year, and I met my goal in 2019. The following techniques are highly influenced by those books; it worked for me, will work for you to.

Writing Income And Expenditure

I made a habit of writing all my income and expenses on a journal and a giant whiteboard in my bedroom. I have found this technique very useful from the fundamental level. First, I can track where my money is going and what portion. Secondly, I can see the actual digits and register them in my subconscious mind. My expense is always lesser than my income. I can see if I am paying a lot of interest on my debt. This writing activity compels me to think about my behavior towards money. I can easily cut the budget on something unnecessary and focus on something more substantial. I do not prefer typing on a computer or phone. I had a student who did not like writing on paper. Instead, he used Microsoft word and a notes pad of his phone for tracking his money. It worked for him. He could also see the worth of almost $86k in his checking account, besides some investments on stocks, 16 months. Only this technique will not open the door for wealth, but this will definitely bring prosperity to your life along with other methods. No training and method I discussed is black magic where you just do this and wealth flows towards you; no, it's not. The reality is, after following my techniques, you start to see the ways to make and multiply your money. Your expenses habit will change. You begin to work smart and know the value of time. One day, I told one of my friends about this method. He refused it. He said that he was able to track his money in credit and debit cards through bank statements. That's true. You may ask me the same question, won't you? If so, why are your expenses habit not changed? How many times in a day or week you look at your income and expenditure statements? Maybe not even a single time. Okay, how about in a month? Maybe once or twice, right? You think your subconscious mind will accept the numbers just by seeing them once or twice a month. You did not know, perhaps, about the subconscious mind then. Now, you know how it works. When you see digits every day, especially, they are the real ones; your income and expenditures, your subconscious mind only recognizes numbers and their associated word, which is money. It won't be able to distinguish between earnings and expenses. When it sees those actual digits repeatedly, it believes that those digits and money are the things on which it has to work. Once the subconscious mind accepts the job, you will shower with money. I mean, whatever you do, you make money. You will be a money-conscious person. The task is more challenging for you to make your subconscious mind believe what you want it to feel, but keep on trying. A persistent person always wins this game.

Reasons To Be Rich

We discussed this topic in goal setting methods too. The secret behind it is similar to the earlier chapter. You need to be very specific about the reasons for you to be rich. Otherwise, the wealth does not stay with you for long. It's like you are planning to get married but has no motivation behind it. You just got married by chance. Then, will you be able to satisfy your partner in different aspects of life? Do you know the reason why another person is in your life? If not, there will be arguments and no respect for each other because you did not have a reason, motivation, and plan for getting married. You will lead a compromised life or get separated. But money does not compromise with you; she will leave you if you do not have any purpose of having her. She will be impressed if the purpose reflects the interest of many people beyond your selfishness. Give a great reason like, for example, you want to be a millionaire because you want to help old people, you want to be a multi-millionaire because you want to build schools and libraries in poor communities, and so on. Make a clear point and be a man of your word when you achieve your desire amount. Do not be like those lottery winners who bankrupted after a few years of winning several million dollars. You can google their names and see that money does not stay with those who do not have a proper reason to be rich.

Lending Money To Friends And Relatives

You may have to reread the phrase; I am saying lending, not helping. There is a proverb that if you want to spoil the relationship with your friends and relatives, lend them money and ask it back in some time. Remember, you are not a bank. Why are you losing money and friendship together? I am not saying you do not help them, but lending and helping are two different topics. The rule of 'helping' is when you are helping someone, you do not expect any assistance or things in return. The moment you want something back for the help you offered, it becomes a business called 'lending.' So, you are doing business with your friends and relatives. The nature of business is to make a profit or loss out of any transaction that occurs. In both ways, whether it is profit or loss, you are not winning anything. From today, stop lending at all. I know you have to be a kind person. When your relatives or friends need you, you have to be there. The technique I tell you over here makes you even kinder and richer in coming times. If it is a life-saving situation, then just help them as much as possible, but you can follow my suggestion in day-to-day cases. Every time my friends and relatives ask me for money, what I do is I give them half of what they ask for and tell them not to worry about paying it back. You may think that it is a 100% loss in that transaction. Why would you do that? There are three specific reasons. First, you will not spoil your relationship. They will always be ready when you actually need them. Moreover, they will connect with you and support you like all branches of the tree. Second, those who you helped will become your strength and power. As time passes, you will pass through various phases of life. You may not need any help right now, but who knows tomorrow? How many people you earned in your life matters the most, and you will understand the connotation of this sentence only when you lay on your death bed. So, save people for the hard times like you are saving money. Third, helping friends and relatives fulfills the quota of donation. We will do a detailed discussion about this in a few seconds.

An Ideal Distribution Of Your Income

I read some classic books about wealth such as 'the richest man in Babylon,' 'the intelligent investor,' and others that gave me an inner insight into the wealth-making process. I created my own model based on those books that I follow every month. My entire paycheck is divided into four parts:

1. **75% of my income** is dedicated to my daily expenses, including groceries, shopping, paying debts if I have, hanging around with friends, etc. If 75% is not enough to maintain my costs, I will work extra and extend the amount that falls in that percentage block. For example, If I make $2500, after-tax, a month, 75% of it will be $1875. This amount has to cover your utilities, gas, internet, phone, health insurance, rent, groceries, clothing, anything you expense on. You have to find a way to adjust within the limit. If you are short of $200 in your budget, you may use other remaining cash. Do not do it. Instead, find a higher-paying job or do some extra hours. You may require another part-time job. If you find a part-time job that pays you $1000, now your 75% of total income will be $2625. With this amount, you will live a little better life than before. If you have extra money remaining, do not save or invest in stocks. Use them for learning or for some training. Enjoy your life. Even if you make a million dollars a month, stick with this model.

2. **10% of your income** should go into a checking account, but you should treat it as a saving account. In the long run, saving hurts your money more; it does not let your money multiply. However, I am telling you to save this amount in checking because life is unpredictable. You may need the cash at any time. If you put it on CD or saving for a specific time limit, you won't be able to withdraw when you need it. If you deposit 10% of your income every month, you will have cash later if you want to go for a vacation or anything you need. When you

use your 10% fund, never use it all; leave some money there. According to the example above, when your income is $2500, you will save $250 every month.

3. **14% of your income** has to go to the investment. This will add up your wealth and expedite your process to be wealthy. If you can adjust your living standard and put more in this block, you can do it. But, never make it less than your saving category. When you start making a profit out of your investment, do not transfer your money to the bank right away. This will cost you money; you will pay more tax, and the financial growth will be minimized. Instead, reinvest the profit. For example, you invested $5000 and, in a few weeks, it becomes $15,000. Do not be greedy and take the money away. When you take the 1st generation profit away from the invested amount, it looks like you are separating a mother from her daughter. You can leave $5000 in the same stock and use the profit for others. If you transfer $10,000 into your bank account, you will pay 22% or more tax which is $2200 in profit. If you reinvest, you will not have to pay that money as a tax right away. Suppose you invested that $10,000 again, and you made $5000 profit on it. You left 5k there in the same stock and reinvested 10k in another that gave you another 3k. You can use this 3k for your expenses because this is the 3rd generation of profit of your invested amount. Unless you make a few generations of profits, you should not eat them up. When a profit gives another profit, I call them a generation of profit. If we analyze the example closely, we can see our net financial growth. For instance, we started with cash 5k. We got a 10k profit that gave us another 5k. The total until now is 20k. We invested 10k that gave us 3k. The final amount we saw is 23k. 5k has become 23k. This is a wrong calculation. Actually, the probability of making more is high here if you have chosen the right stocks. I tell you how. We got 10k as profit that was reinvested in different stock, but 5k is still there, generating more money. That the mother of all

profits, and she is still in the market. Another capital we forgot is 5k from the second generation, which was still making money along with her mother, initial 5k, and her daughter-profit, 5k. When you transferred 3k to your bank, 10k was still working. So, overall, the mother capital 5k was working, daughter profit 10k was working, grand-daughter profit 5k was still working, daughter profit 10k has given birth to two daughter profits that are 5k and 3k. So, the total yield cannot be counted in our example because the stock market fluctuates so much and is volatile. However, according to the flowing our model, the total profit will be more than 23k for sure.

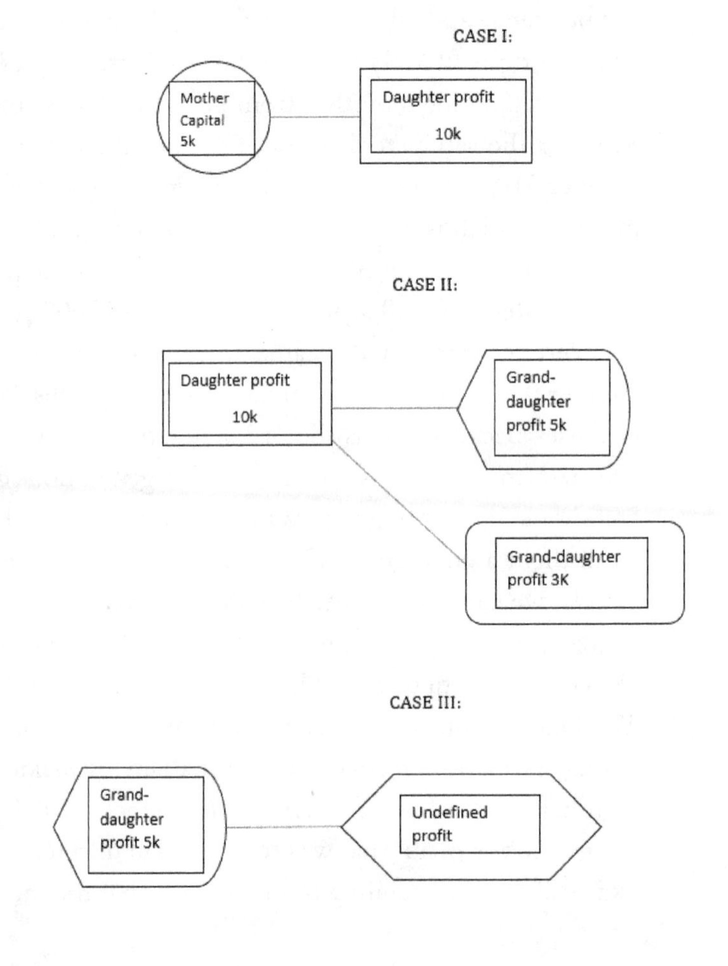

The charts above show that mother capital 5k was still working while case II is happening. While case III was going on, mother capital was working, daughter profit 10k was working, and the last gain we have not included yet. Thus, in this way, we would make more money when we deploy our profits instead of killing them. This is called hiring cash for your business. If this technique is used in real estate, renting apartments and houses, there is always an enormous profit. An ordinary person with a capital of 80k can be a multi-millionaire in 5 years with the understanding of this model and principle of wealth.

4. **1% is separated for donation.** Have you ever noticed that all religions in the world encourage us to donate some of our income? I know most of you are not religious but spiritual like me, who do not care what certain religions say. However, those people who came up with such a divine idea must have seen and experienced its outcome. Donation is the most appeasing act you can do to yourself. You donate to others but get satisfaction to yourself. You donate food to the hungry; you get full by itself. If we take our previous example to see the actual donation amount, it will be $25 every month. This is not a life-changing amount, but if you add it up for the year, you will have $300. Now, this amount can really bring many changes in the poor communities of a poor country. Make a habit of donating to the poor where your small amount would be converted into much more. Sometimes, the expensive cost of your coffee can be enough to pay the rent of an entire month for someone living in a different part of the globe; never underestimate the change you can bring to the life of others.

It is not easy to donate internationally because several crocked people act as mediators and take away all money. You will never find it that whether he facilitated the cash to the right person or not. I experienced this twice. You need to be very careful about donating.

When you donate, never ever seek any public reputation or fame. When you do it for fame, donation becomes an act of business; you gave money, and they gave you fame. No, you do not want it. Do not tell anyone that you are donating. Taking pictures or making videos while donating is the worst trend I see nowadays. It is good in one sense that people may get motivated with your act and start doing the same. However, the real benefits you would be receiving from the universe will be nullified. Do not trade your hard work money for that cheap social media fame.

Talking about part C, in the example, you gave half of the money that your friends and relative asked for, and you told them not to pay it back. If the amount falls under 1%, you can assume that you donated the amount to your friend. If it is more than the donation percentage, you have to find an ideal way to fix the issue. If you make $2500 per month in real life and think about donating $10k yearly, you need to wake up from the dream because you violate the model and principle of wealth.

Focus On Passive Income

The principal nature of humans is to be free. We like to be able to do what we want whenever we want. If we look at a child of 4-5 years old, he is the master of his will; he can sleep, run, cry, laugh, and be stubborn to achieve what he wants. There is no stress at all. He has limited knowledge about the life and suffering that humanity has created to entangle itself. He does not bother to waste time thinking about where the food is coming from or the procedure to cook it. Only the thing that matters to him is the freedom of everything he wants. There is no way that we can get such space throughout our life. However, we must strive for it, and every single minute living in a free state of mind counts. The biggest thing that enslaving the vast majority of the human population is 'JOB'; working for somebody. We work hard daily to train or educate ourselves to prove ourselves as better servants or slaves. Our masters give us more benefits and affections if we diligently obey them. Nobody forces anyone to fall into this trend, but a man is bound by the social structure, which designs the labour that society needs. From school and college, a person is trained to be laborious. In higher studies, they pick the industry where they will be working for most of their life. Most of us keep on switching the job. I know many people who spent 5-7 years training and studying in specific fields, but they get tired as soon as they start working in that field. Some people cannot live without complaining about their jobs. I have a lot of friends who get stressed on Sunday because they have to work on Monday. I used to have the same feeling when I was working for some company. Most people get stressed around the time when they have to leave for the job. Even if the job is from home, most of us are unhappy to work. I am not saying that nobody is happy by working a 9 to 5 job. Some people prepare themselves for a dream job. But careers take away our freedom. Most part of our day is spent making somebody else rich and happy. We do not get days off when we want. We do not get appreciated for our job as much as we deserve. A few hundred additional bucks can be noticed in the pay check when the promotion happens, but it brings so much hidden stress and responsibilities. If you want to travel, you have to plan once a year and in advance. Even after that, you cannot stay as much as you want abroad. Life is so much narrowed and tied with so many chins. To break those chains, we have to find a way to make enough money without getting involved in the money-making process actively. When I did research about the sources of passive income, I found them worthwhile in trying. Most of them do not relate to many of us because they talk about many investments and capital. However, I have experienced that if one desires to achieve something intensely, the entire universe works to bring them, the person and his desires, together. Some of the topics I found in my research are:

1. **Writing a book:** This is a very effective way to make some passive income. Writers can make royalty throughout his life without doing anything. The print-on-demand option has given an excellent opportunity to any writer to sell his books

without printing in advance. This means no investment before the sale. If you are good at writing and advertising, you can make your fortune in these fields as well. You will have to work hard once, and it may pay you back for a long time. The book such as Rich dan and poor dad, people still love it after more than 20 years of its publication. The information in the book is unchanged, but it is reappearing in the market every year, providing a good amount of royalty to the author. The royalty can be varied for traditional publish and self-publish. If you go through traditional publishers, the rates may be as follows:

eBook sales: 25%
Paperback copy: 7%
Hardcover copy: 15%
Audiobook: 25%

If you go through self-publish, you may get higher royalty for eBooks, between 35% - 70%. For paperback and other formats, you get paid as long as your books are getting sold. There are many writers I know who have published several books and still made from their first one. It's on you how are going to use your creativity in making money but remember that everyone can **WRITE.**

2. **Blogging:** Some people take this hobby as a full-time job. The difference between this job and other day jobs is making money while sleeping by blogging. When your website is visited by thousands of viewers in an hour, you make a good amount of money. I know someone who makes above 20k per month just by blogging. You can connect your website with AdSense to pay you extra when people buy stuff through your website. The topic you wrote about 10 years ago will continue serving you money while asleep or chilling with your friends and family.

3. **YouTube:** Who does not know about this? We all know that this technology has helped millions of people across the globe make their lives. In many countries today, people watch YouTube for news and information more than their national television channels. Since there is no registration or account initiation fee, all sorts of people are actively getting into this field. While doing research, I found a guy who became a multi-millionaire in 4 years just by uploading videos of him playing video games. I have several engineers and scientist friends; they make barely 8k per month by working more than 40 hours a week and bearing tons of load on their shoulders. A Vlogger makes above 10k in a month by visiting different places and enjoying his life; he is not bound by the rules and instructions of his boss. This platform actually gives you money, name, and fame.

4. **Social media:** We all have some social media accounts. Social media is the most fantastic concept of connecting people from all around the world. People make thousands and thousands of dollars through these platforms. We might have heard about Instagram models, famous Tiktokers, or Facebook influencers who make a lot of money by doing what they find interesting to them. You can sell products on these platforms. I saw a teenager charging restaurant owners 1k per month for simply posting a picture of their food on his social media. He had more than 20 customers. That means he was making more than 20k. I had a student who did her business thoroughly on Facebook. She used to make a lot more than she could make from her engineering job. When you have many followers on Tiktok or Instagram, try to do some business out of it; put some product or endorse some product and make passive income.

5. **Stocks:** This one is the most volatile. I cannot guarantee that you will make some passive income out of it because a business

can bankrupt, and you may lose your investment. If you spend enough time learning and getting associated with other experienced investors, the risk is minimum. If you follow the technique, I discussed earlier reinvesting your profit, you may see the growth of wealth faster. I suggest people put money in stocks if they have plenty of it and leave some alone. Otherwise, this investment gets you stuck for a good long time unless you sell them, taking the loss. But, the 1st law of money is 'never lose it.' You will violate the law. If there is an alternative place to invest, such as a real business, I would prefer investing there rather than in the stocks. However, the stock market is where your money works for you, even if you are not aware of it. I have experienced so much positivity in investing in stocks.

6. **Airbnb or renting your house:** If you have a home and there is a spare room, you can try Airbnb or renting it out. I had 3 roommates living in the house from whom I used to make $1900. On the other hand, if you are living in a good community, your home gets appraised. In my case, before I paid my first mortgage, the house appraised by 40k, and in one and a half years, the price got almost double. This roommate idea gave me extra-economic freedom, and I had plenty of time for my upcoming books and a business plan that I have been working for a long.

7. **Real estate:** This is my first choice if I have to pick one to be wealthy but to get into this business, we need budget, training, and mentor if possible. People make money by flipping the properties, too, but I prefer to rent it out. I studied so many books regarding this business and attended a few pieces of training. Making several million dollars from a million is a lot easier than making 100k out of 1k. All real estate books give you the idea of making millions from a million but do not tell us the procedure to make a million out of 100k or less.

In the tour of middle east in 2019, I met a man who owned 23 units and made almost 20k as passive income. That was the amount he was receiving after the deduction of all expenses related to the properties. I asked him the procedure of how he managed to do it, and he told me that he started all of those from 70k. His trick was finding some bank-owned houses, foreclosures houses, or the places put on sale by the county. The reason behind it was those houses were so cheap. The first duplex he bought cost him around 30k. He invested 40k more in renovating it and put it on the market for rent. Very soon, the house got occupied, and he started making money from two apartments. Then, he decided to replicate his procedure to buy more homes, but he did not have money left. So, he went to the bank, showed the paperwork owning the house, and asked for a loan. The bank soon approved 90k because the market value of the house was more than 155k. If he had flipped the house, his net profit would be more than 85k. When he received the loan, the rent amount was more than enough to pay for the loan; he found another house and put on rent again. This time he saw a great deal; he had a four plexus. Now, the income was more because he had 6 units generating cash. The money was flooding towards him, and he could do the same tricks under his wife's name. Finally, they were able to make more than 20k as passive income every month.

The process of making money should be easy and less time-consuming. Otherwise, you will spend your entire life collecting cash, and one day when you run out of time, you will realize that you did not live life to the fullest. Money is extremely important to lead a happy and healthy life but do not work hard to make somebody else richer and more potent. Instead, find your strength and work on yourself.

1. **Own business:** This is the most time-consuming thing. However, instead of working 12 hours a day for someone else, I would prefer working 15 hours a day for myself. Though it seems like it is taking away a lot of time initially, you will enjoy your economic freedom sooner or later if you sustain in the

market for long. However, human is greedy by nature. Thus, you may end up working 18 hours every day even after being successful in establishing your business. Once you start making some cash flow, invest in something else to help you achieve your economic freedom revolution. If you are thinking about opening 3-4 different businesses, I would suggest opening something related to each other. I know many business advisors suggest investing in different areas with no connection, but I have a different feeling. For example, you run a gas station and invest in book stores as another income source. These two are entirely different from each other though you can put some books in a gas station as a display to sell them out. For a book store, a publication house would be the right helping business. I would instead get a liquor license which is more compatible with the gas station. My point is if you are opening several companies, they need to have targeted customers. If you are yourself a customer then, the loss is minimized. I mean, you have a liquor store, and you open a beer factory. Another one, you can open a bar as well. In this example, you have a liquor store, beer factory, and a bar; all of them are related to each other. It is like you are the manufacturing company, and you are the source of raw materials, and you are the one who is taking the product into the market or to the customers. In this type of interrelated business, you do not have to depend on vendors to run your factory. It is just an example.

It seems like this entire chapter is detected in the materialistic world. What is the role of money in spirituality? In today's world, money is not everything, but to get everything, we need money. If we look at the history of meditation that goes thousands of years before Buddha, people always meditated to attain power, wealth, knowledge, and kingdom. The concept of abandoning everything and attaining enlightenment is not only the path of spirituality. You can meditate while being super-rich, or you can meditate to be super-rich. This is not my opinion; this is the fact we can read in Upanishads or Puranas. There is so many historical and mythical individual such as Ravana who meditated years to become the king of the entire earth. There are so many other names who meditated to be super powerful and wealthy. Thus, the concept such as you have to sell your belongings to be a monk is new. I think people started copying Buddha in the hope of attaining enlightenment by renouncing their social status, friends, and relatives. I am not questioning the path because, as we all know, Siddhartha Gautam Buddha is a very successful monk in the spiritual world. We consider him as God or a person with godly character. But not everyone can become Buddha, and renouncing is not only the meditation method. Love, affection, and sympathy are the by-product of meditation. But it does not mean that all yogis or meditators should not get mad or do not get angry. Lord Shiva is revered as 'Adi yogi,' the first yogi who introduced meditation into our society several thousand years ago. Upanishads and Puranas explain how quick lord shiva gets mad and be pleased. The misconceptions about meditation nowadays are that you have to be disconnected from everything to connect with God. Who has seen God? Has anyone taken a selfie with God after reaching to him? So, you are willing to sacrifice people and things that are real and in front of you to meet someone whose existence is questionable. There is nothing wrong with being wealthy; do not sell your stuff to attain so-called peace. The peace is there even if you do not sell your properties to be a monk. Otherwise, you only get a placebo effect of believing, 'I did just like buddha, now I will be next buddha.' There is no guarantee that the same path in spirituality will lead you to the same destination. You pick your own path. I showed you the truth, and I am repeating again that people constantly meditated to receive wealth, power, wife/ husband, kingdom, lands, physical strength, control over others, etc., in the past. If you want to meditate for your material desires, you can go ahead, but your desire to get wealthy may change into becoming wiser after a few years of practice. However, there is no problem in meditating for such desires until you follow the wealth model and help the poor.

Summary Of Chapter VII

We have been brainwashed about the information of money and wealth. Since childhood, we are told that money is evil, and we have always condemned wealthy people. We are told all beautiful stories that support Pluto-phobia, phobia of wealth. Those people who have never experienced the poverty, are the one who is writing on the experiences of poverty. We must change the trend and pattern of our way of thinking; nothing wrong with being rich. When we become rich, so many people associated with us will benefit too. An extremely poor cannot help another poor creating anyone's happy life; if a blind leads another blind, both shall fall into the ditch. We can bring changes in society only if we bring changes within ourselves. Meditation will help us in seeing the opportunity in financial deals, and it can eradicate poverty. Meditation does not require anyone to renounce his belongings. Instead, meditation always helps to create a good relationship of everything together. We can be wealthy as well as a monk at the same time. Society has a false image of yogis. People want yogi or meditators to be poor and emaciated, which is deluding and completely fallacious. If meditation makes you poor, gaunt, powerless, and less energy, then there is no need for it. But in reality, meditation offers strength, power, wealth, and fame. This is why meditation is still in practice and surviving several thousand years as a practice. Whereas a lot of other aspects of ancient lifestyle have perished. Try on yourself first; meditate, become rich, help others, donate more, and if you still do not get happiness, meet those who abandoned everything to get something. Finally, make the right decision, whichever is good for you.

1. **Wake-up: 6 A.M.**
2. **Drink water, sip by sip.**
3. **Write dream tracking journal.**
4. **Drink the boiled water with my recipe.**
5. **Practice deep breathing in an open area.**
6. **Chant the mantra you created.**
7. **Physical exercise, flexibility, and Chess game**
8. **Practice visualization (does not have to be in the morning).**
9. **Be kind, and practice the willpower in as many activities as possible.**
10. **Eat healthy and detach yourself from unnecessary desires.**
11. **Exercises to find the reason of your existence.**
12. **Change your attitude towards the money.**
13. **Self-hypnosis before bed/anytime.**
14. **Chant the mantra you created before bed.**

CHAPTER VIII

THE COURAGE

"The secret of happiness is freedom and the secret to freedom is courage."- Thucydides

Sometimes you just need to be brave. If you act soft all the time, people find you fragile and try to break you in every possible way. As we know, all straight trees are cut down first in the forest. To live in society, we need to be harsh, or people take advantage of our softness. Have you ever been chased by stray dogs? The more you run, the more they chase. Only the way to scare them is showing some courage and stepping towards them. Once you stop and move towards them, they get scared and move backward. Also, the ferocious animals like cheetah, tiger, and bear get afraid of. Actually, all living beings get so frightened of other more enormous beings. That is because of a default application downloaded in our subconscious mind and the fear of death. We all living creatures want to live a total length of life or as long as possible. As a result, when we sense we are in danger, our default function starts reacting and thus, activates the mode of fight or flee. By default, 'flee' is the safest and easiest one. So, we prefer running away from the danger. This is the nature of our innate instinct. Fight mode starts when flee does not work, but fight mode does not last long unless there is a practice of courage in life so often. A dog that is aggressive most of the time has a high chance of scaring more giant animals like a tiger than a dog that is docile by nature.

Being courageous is a higher energy level state. This is why it is not easy to sustain at that level all the time. On the other hand, we do not require to be courageous every step of our life. We should definitely avoid aggression as much as possible, but we should never delete it forever because anger helps bring up the courage. Courage without rage is like a car without fuel. We should not destroy the anger; instead, we need to control it. When something is under control, you can bring it to use whenever you want. If you completely destroy it, theoretically, you will run out of it. But there is no way that we would be able to annihilate anger anyway. Some people may have an enormous level of patience. However, if one is provoked enough, he will get mad. We need to train ourselves to amplify our anger and use it in the right place in a proper way.

When you are spiritual and saint by nature, you may not be bothered by many daily issues, but there are some inhuman activities by seeing which your opinion may change. If you look at the history of Sanatan dharma, you see many sages have picked up weapons to save the innocents. If meditation makes you a coward, you are following the wrong methods. Of course, meditation makes you more tolerant, forgiving, and caring, but everything has a limit. You feel it when the boundary is crossed. Most people suffer because they do not dare to take action at the right time. We are controlled by our fears, a fear of losing something. Fear does not allow us to be courageous. We must overcome our fear to be free. When something terrible is happening in society, we don't dare to protest it. We are scared to speak the truth against some influential people. We consider ourselves weak when putting ourselves physically into the fights to save somebody else. We tend to be wise and avoid such commotion. Everyone has at least one opportunity to demonstrate personal courage in his lifetime, but most of us ignore it for our safety. The courage I am talking about is something life-saving or taking or at least doing something risky to bring change but not daring to approach a pretty girl or act of bungee jumping. For example, you saw a group of men attempting rape to a minor at midnight in an isolated place, and suppose that you do not have a cell phone. What would you do as a spiritual person? I know all of you think you would intervene. But thinking and doing are different things. The thing that makes a difference in them is courage. If you have real courage, you will put yourself in danger to rescue the girl or at least do not flee from the site. It is easy to imagine, but when it comes to our own life, we tremble. In reality, most people ignore the scenario and flee from the site. Until it does not happen to our family or us, we prefer ignoring the situation. We do not get mad when the problem is not hurting us, and we are not a part of the issue. If there is fear instead of anger, how can personal courage sprout?

I remember an incident where I put myself into the situation. This is the incident that occurred when I was in 10th standard. There was construction work on a house going on in our neighborhood. A couple was living in that uncompleted house as caretakers of the site. One day, when I got back from school, I saw a lady with swollen face talking to another woman. She was crying. Usually, I do not be nosy and always swim in my own lane, but I was curious to know why she was crying that day. Her husband was physically abusing her every day. She mentioned that her husband brings prostitutes into the room, and if she objects, he beats her brutally. I felt very uncomfortable hearing that, and I left. Later in the evening, I was studying in my room, and my mother was making food in the kitchen. Suddenly, we heard a scream of female voice. I was a little bit agitated. My mom came to my room and told me that the guy was hitting his wife again. I decided to go outside. I saw a lot of people watching from everywhere; window, balcony, door, and courtyard. I felt pretty bad and hoped someone, older people, would take action. I went back to my room for the preparation of the test. After a few minutes, I heard a loud noise or bang on the wall. My mom came to my room and told me what was happening there. I peeked from the window; I could not see anything but heard the lady weeping. I told my mom that I was going to get involved, but she objected.

My hands and legs were shaking; I still remember the moments. My mind could not think anything; otherwise, a boy of 15 years old would not dare to fight with a man twice his age. I went outside, ran towards the man, and pushed him on the ground very hard. Before he was on his feet, I held his neck and hurled him on the floor again. He fell 3-4 feet away from me. I used my elbow to hit behind his neck. I did not allow him to realize what was happening to him. Very soon, apologized. I said, "She, referring to his wife, is my sister. If anything happens to her, I am going to kill you." My voice was quavering while saying that with anger. My mother dragged me to my room. My hands and legs were still shaking; I was outraged. Many people enjoyed the moments, but nobody decided to protect the lady or help a kid fight. If I knew he had been beating his wife from the beginning, I would never let it happen.

I was busy in school, and the construction was already completed. Thus, I did not see the couple for a few months. One day after 6 months of that incident, I met a lady in a different town. I almost had forgotten her. She reminded me of the incident to introduce herself. After I fought with her husband and called her my sister, she said he never mistreated or abused her. She was so glad. She blessed me with her heart. I did not expect that change in her husband, but it had to be true if she told me. I cannot explain how you feel when someone's life changes because of your action. That was only the fight I got involved in. I have many other incidents where I used verbal strength to mitigate or eradicate the tensions between people. Fighting may not be the solution for many cases, but there is no option or better replacement for it in some cases.

There is a story of a Gurkha soldier, Bishnu Shrestha, who fought 40 robbers to save an 18 years old girl from being raped. He only had a Nepali knife with him to fight against 40 robbers and their rifles. It happened in September of 2010 when he was returning from India to Nepal on the break. He was a soldier in the Indian Gurkha regiment. When the robbers intruded on the train, he was asleep. All passengers were already looted, and he was ready to hand over his belongings to robbers too. Suddenly some of the robbers grabbed an 18 years girl in a rape attempt. Then, he decided to fight against the group of 40 men. They shot at him but missed him. He severely injured many of them. Finally, robbers gave up and started escaping the scene. Six of them were arrested. Bishnu received a Medal for bravery. This incident also tells us that courage is driven by anger. If there was no anger in him, he would not be motivated to fight. A soldier without rage is like a snake without venom. His wrath did not show up until robbers intended to mistreat a girl.

The courage I am talking about definitely promotes bravery, but it contains violence in it, and that violence is inevitable for the welfare of many innocents. Some incidents are not like getting slapped on one check and putting forward another. Suppose person A attempts to rape or murder, and you saw it at the right time. You do not have time to call anyone for help, but you can hit the guy from the back. Will, you hit him? It may kill the person. No matter what, it is violence, whether he kills someone or you kill him. You may get away from the legal issues for defending the victim. What does spirituality say about this? This is not a question from today or yesterday; people have always asked such questions in the history of spirituality because the philosophy of spirituality and meditation sometimes seems to be tricky and contradictory, if not understood completely.

In some cases, we are advised to take action and, in some, just to view the world with 'Drasta bhava.' But when a person has a better understanding of philosophy, he will know what to do. A book was published in 2004 on 'The Mahabharat, Volume 7' by Fitzgerald James. He showed in his work that in some situations, following violence is the best way to prevent the greater violence that can take the lives of many. In such a case, not killing someone may lead to a greater catastrophe. He mentioned, ".....tradition teaches that the fault in killing one who should not be killed is the same as not killing one who should be killed" (Fitzerald, 2004). Arjuna had the same dilemma

(Bhagwat Geeta); why kill his own relatives.

Krishna advised him that killing is the duty of soldiers, no matter who is standing against him. So, Krishna suggests that we should to be 'Dharma Yoddha,' a person who performs his duty at any cost. Mahatma Gandhi said, "Ahimsa (nonviolence) is an ideal which it is impossible to realize to perfection. It may be possible to realize it in thought, but not always in action."

All religions and cultures teach us to be sympathetic and caring. They also talk about God punishing the sin committer. Sometimes, we do not have enough time to wait for God or anyone to punish them; we have to move forward and do what is right. My intention in this chapter is nothing else but to make you feel okay if you injured or killed someone who is attempting rape to your daughter, sister, or mother. Meditation has to give that physical and mental power to protect one's family and himself. Your wife/husband or daughter/son should feel safe and protected when you are around.

Be Fearless

Our mind is clustered with many fears. The fear of uncertainty agitates the peaceful state of mind. Our future is uncertain. We keep on thinking and worrying about our coming days. We always hope for better, but the hope does not assure us of any better future. Either you believe that you can design your own destiny or think that the future already exists, but you cannot deny its existence. The future is unpredictable because it is influenced by our activities and that of others. If only my activities determined my fate, I would imitate someone like Einstein. I would have similar personalities by copying someone, which does not confirm my success similarly as I am imitating. The future is determined by the collective mind. Einstein's theory of relativity allows time travel, but with his method, we can travel only in the future, not in the past. So, this means the future is already in existence. The future is determined by our actions in the present. The present is the only one that is present in the past and the future both. Yesterday was also a present moment for that day, and the coming day will no longer be the future tomorrow. Whether we can see the future or not, if we see our present with open eyes and presence of mind, the future will definitely be the pleasant one. We should be mindful about what we see, do, and think in the present.

If we do something great every day, we do not require waiting for our happiness. The future cannot scare us then. If the reason for our fear is a physical matter or creature, there is no other way around it than to fight it. Some people often mistake being rude as being fearless. Hurting somebody's feelings by telling unnecessary bitter truth is an act of courage for them. This kind of impractical thinking always creates irritation in people, and you will have to live in fear; you are making new enemies every day. To be fearless does not mean taking unnecessary risks. Passing comments on somebody's character will not make you a good person, even if it is true. Besides, jumping into the cage of a wild animal is also not fearless. Staying away from the stress of the future, the feeling of what others say, challenging myself, freeing myself from the grief of past, forgiving others for their forgivable deeds, never accepting defeat, etc. are the example of being fearless my definition. Find your own appropriate definition and be courageous.

Making A Decision

We often decide for the peace of our mind, but we should make decisions with peace of mind. When something or someone hurts us, we become emotional; we will lose our mind's peace and become more fragile. Since it is the most painful time, we continuously seek peace, which may create many blunders. At present, it may look fine, but in time, such decisions will hurt us more. For example, when someone is separated from his beloved after a terrible breakup or divorce, he will lose his peace of mind. He tends to get into another relationship to tame the mind and get some affection for the burning heart. If he makes a decision within a short interval of time after the divorce, that decision is the outcome of his relentless mind. There is a high chance for him to regrate in the future about the decision. Always make decisions when you are in the calmest state of mind.

Struggle And Hardship

Life needs struggles to grow to its full potential. The hindrances on our paths in achieving success or happiness, the failures, and losses we encounter, the pains and diseases we survive, etc., are nothing else than chisel and hammer trying to sculpt our life more beautiful. The more hit from it, the more beautiful life turns out to be. If somebody is sculpting a statue, he will hit the stone from all sides. After getting hit thousand times and getting chipped off more than half of itself, a rock becomes a beautiful statue. A statue is not utterly satisfactory until it is carved or sculpted from all sides. Likewise, when the situations hit us from all sides, we become more precious. It is easy to imagine that we can overcome any struggles that come our way because we know that we grow stronger and become precious after that. But in real life, our brain stops thinking when a series of hardships strike us. As a result, many of us become the victim of depression and some gives up and takes his life. It requires an extreme level of destructive thought to kill oneself because suicide is a violation of the principle of life. Naturally, by default, no organism wants to destroy itself, and the programming installed in our subconscious mind promotes life.

When a person is suicidal, he is constantly thinking about the way of ending his life. He becomes successful in confusing the subconscious mind. As a result, the situation he wants will be created. However, that does not mean that the default program of our mind did not work. When the default program does not work, the internal systems stop functioning. It is possible for yogi only. It is known as 'Swa Ikchha Mrityu Varan' means 'death on self-desire. This is not suicide. Neither do you hurt yourself in this process; it is the process of calming down each and every part of our body, stopping the functioning of every cell, and completely erasing the programs from our minds. This is the ability to successfully override the system and delete the programs responsible for unconscious activities like blood circulation, body temperature, heartbeat, etc. I watched a live video of a Buddhist monk in Myanmar who left his body upon his will. A few seconds ago, he seemed fine and then walked towards an arranged death bed, coffin and laid on to it. In a few minutes, his body stops functioning; no heat, no circulation, and no breathing. Then, other monks carried him for cremation. He was gone that easy. I have read several stories of people practicing meditation who has this power.

However, this is the act of another level of consciousness. For a suicidal person, his constant appearing negative thoughts overpower the default program of life. If we can override the default program just by having a continual thought, why don't we think about the progressive life? Living with the full potential of life is not against the subconscious mind. But our polluted conscious mind is on the way. Everything we see is manipulated and judged based on the data available in our conscious minds. This database is collected through our experiences, and we experience our surrounding nature. Our surrounding is influenced with stupid minds and all negativities. Everything we know is dipped in the ocean of negativity. We really need to practice to see a good part of everything we encounter daily. But the reality is, people see something wrong in all good things. When the situation is not in our favor, we tremble, and the pleasure is not pleasant anymore. The experiences of things change. We slowly degrade. When challenges and hard times come, or we know it's impending, we try to find a way around rather than get through it. We miss some hits of chisel and hammer. As a result, some sides of our life remain unfinished and ugly. If you want to be attractive from all sides of life, you need to take all hits and pass through the challenges that life offers; be courageous to accept challenges. Never give up: never accept defeat and never quit.

Imagination

If there is someplace where you can find the purest positive information, it is your imaginative world. Unfortunately, many people underestimate the power of this world and pollute it with their negativities. Once Einstein said, "Imagination is more important than knowledge. Knowledge is limited. Imagination encircles the world." He was considered an underperforming student in his childhood, but that did not stop him from imagining the world he liked. If you want to drop or increase your body temperature for an experiment, how you do it? Simply, by Imagination. Imagine as if you were covered with ice or walking in a snowy place; your temperature drops. This one is a little harder practice. Imagine you are licking a half-cut lemon; your mouth will be filled with saliva immediately. You imagined the process, but your body took it as a real act and created enzymes and more saliva to start the digestion process. See, it is not that hard to fool the conscious mind. What causes a panic attack?

According to USA Today magazine, "biochemical reactions such as increased adrenaline levels in the body or any hormonal imbalance is one of the reasons for a panic attack." Besides, some suppressed emotions, childhood hardship, or unconscious conflicts from the past can be a reason for the issue. Does a panic attack have something to do with Imagination? When something triggers our past experiences, a person's mind reacts as it is happening in the present. Our brain gets tricked and releasees the related hormones, stress, or happy hormone. When the brain cannot differentiate reality from Imagination, our entire system reacts to emotions. If painful experiences can give us panic attacks and anxiety, why don't blissful experiences take us in a more bliss state? Why does negativity have more strength than positivity to impact our mind and body? Strangely, we are more likely to be negative or more chances to believe in negativity.

Similarly, after a few repetitions, when we start a harmful activity, it becomes a habit, but a good lifestyle barely becomes a habit. For example, not going gym twice can beat the habit of going gym every day. Science says it takes roughly 21 days to form a habit, but I woke up at 3:50 A.M. every day, without a break, for 10 months, still did not become a habit. I still have the same motivation and goal to wake up early. However, the habit was broken. In those 10 months of waking up early, I never felt like it became my habit because I had to force myself to wake up early, and I did because of my promise; I had some goals to achieve. On the contrary, if you sleep 10 hours a day for 10 days, it is more likely to become your habit. Are we designed to be lazy? Definitely not. Then, what makes it easier to accept something not good as our habit? This good and bad is the matter of the conscious mind, and making a habit is the task of the subconscious mind. Clearly, the subconscious mind does not know the difference between good and bad. On the other hand, making a habit depends on the vibration. We can force ourselves to vibrate in some energy level for a certain time, but eventually, we are more likely to fall back to our original state. When I was waking up early in the morning, at 3:50 A.M., I was forcing myself to vibrate in that energy level. If you research the lifestyle of CEOs of big companies and most successful people, you will see that they are waking up very early, around that time. I had similar goals as they had when I was waking up early that helped vibrate in their energy level. As soon as my goal was completed, I fell down to my original level. It is tough to continue it because my mind's situation makes it impossible to continue such a schedule. For example, when I was buying a house, I required a full-time job. After getting out of the Army, I decided never to work for someone else unless it is required for my life objectives. I started working a random shift; day, evening, and night. Those four months of job destroyed a year-old habit of waking up early.

If your goal requires such a tough schedule of bed and wake-up time, you will have a strong reason to wake up early, and eventually, you will be able to create a habit of waking up early. In my case, I was in a hostile environment, 2nd deployment in the Middle East, where the temperature and other pressures prevailed. We used to have incoming every other week at a random time. Maybe because of such unpredictable factors, my mind could not set the schedule as a habit. The maximum hour, if I had slept any day in 2019, was 5 hours 50 min. regardless of the weekends or celebrations. To become something as a habit, your brain should excrete happy hormones such as dopamine, oxytocin, endorphins, and serotonin as the reaction of your certain action. When you do something, you should feel good. The action can be pleasant or not, but your mind should release a pleasant-related hormone. For example, poking someone with a needle is a painful act, but people addicted to tattoos love it. A drug addict skips the feeling of pain, does not care about it from a needle while injecting the drug. It is all about the chemicals. If you want to establish a habit, you will have to establish a relationship of your happiness with it. When the reality is too harsh, your Imagination will work for this process. If you are working on a difficult project of your life, creating a new habit, or quitting the undesired one, use your power of Imagination; imagine that you already have your desired habit and visualize the happiness related to it. You need to feel it in depth and construct a strong bridge between your goal and the feelings so that you can order your brain to excrete the hormones when you want. This will motivate you constantly to reach out for success in your life.

However, if you are just daydreaming, your 1conscious mind will block the signal reaching the brain to excretes hormones sooner or later. Instead, it may release stress hormones. There is a difference between daydreaming and higher Imagination. Daydreaming lacks directions, and no action would be taken to process it in the physical world. While daydreaming, a person knows he is wasting time. You need to imagine vivid with logic. It has to be a mental rehearsal rather than a random play of thoughts. Each and every character in thought should fulfill their role. Yes, Imagination can be considered a play; our brain is the auditorium, thoughts are the characters, the conscious mind is the director/ editor, and other levels of minds are the board of directors to decide whether the play is convincing enough to pass into the materialistic world. They do not decide the worthiness of play based on good or evil; they check on the realistic aspect. Not all characters mean thoughts, get roles all the time, and some get denied, but the play goes on. We should be able to send the same character repeatedly if we want it to be a character of the play. Our senses are the door's way to collect those characters to send them to the auditorium. If we see or be around positivity, those positive characters will get the opportunity to take part in the play. If they get denied for the roles, we need to be persistent by being positive all the time. Be imaginative.

Summary Of Chapter VIII

Our responsibilities are not only limited to ourselves. We simply cannot choose to escape the situation when our family and friends are in trouble. Even animals dare to rescue their herd members from the midst of a beast. We must be able to make decisions with courage when time demands it. We cannot follow nonviolence in every step of life; sometimes, the situation worsens than getting slapped on one cheek. If somebody slaps on our cheek, we can put forward another, but if someone rapes one of our daughters, we cannot bring forward another daughter in front of the rapist. A courageous person definitely fights to save their children and family. No daughter deserves a cowardly father; neither anyone does. Be unafraid to take an appropriate step for yourself and your community. We have limitless hindrances and struggles in our life. People may try to break you down. Do not be disheartened. The more challenges you over, the stronger you will be. Life is beautiful when it is hit by problems from all sides. You will turn out to be a three-dimensional statue. When the reality is too bitter, you need to remember that the play is going in the brain. When your desired thought does not get to be a part of the play, you should continue sending such thoughts to the auditorium.

One day, the play director will get tired of seeing the same character begging for the role repeatedly. He will hire your feelings for the play. As a result, your thoughts turn into reality in the outside, material world. Thus, never underestimate the power of Imagination, which can create reality.

1. **Wake-up: 6 A.M.**
2. **Drink water, sip by sip.**
3. **Write dream tracking journal.**
4. **Drink the boiled water with my recipe.**
5. **Practice deep breathing in an open area.**
6. **Chant the mantra you created.**
7. **Physical exercise, flexibility, and Chess game**
8. **Practice visualization (does not have to be in the morning).**
9. **Be kind, and practice the willpower in as many activities as possible.**
10. **Eat healthy and detach yourself from unnecessary desires.**
11. **Exercises to find the reason of your existence.**
12. **Change your attitude towards the money.**
13. **Be courageous.**
14. **Self-hypnosis before bed/anytime.**
15. **Chant the mantra you created before bed.**

CHAPTER IX

READING

"Employ your time in improving yourself by other men's writings so that you shall come easily by what others have laboured hard for." - Socrates

Some moths are driven by positive phototaxis; they hover over the fire repeatedly. They do not learn from their own experiences and get immolated. Animals such as dogs will scare to come back to you if you show your hatred toward them; they learn from their experiences. Some animals, such as monkeys and octopuses, learn by watching. Humans neither need their own experiences nor require to watch any demonstrations; they can learn from reading. The easiest way to get knowledge about anything in detail is by reading. Books are the outcome of the life-long learning process of authors. Most of the life-changing books we see today are the collection of the author's own experiences. These authors take an entire life to write a book, but we can read and understand it within few days. We really do not have to go through each and every situation that writers went through to understand his finding. Many people boast about their life-handling skills and comment saying a book cannot teach the fundamental skill of life or books are limited in the paper only. It really depends on what you are reading. If you are reading about swimming without going into the water, the book won't teach you such skills. Even the world's best swimmer cannot teach you swimming without a pool, river, or lake. If you want to be a surgeon, you must practice dissecting wounds; reading the book 'how to cut a wound' cannot make you courageous enough to tackle with fear of blood and injury. If you look at the past or present, you will find all successful people read books no matter their field. Books are the best friends of a wise person. They can motivate anyone and change the thinking pattern of a person. Reading habits not only make us more intelligent by providing information but also shape our brains. Many parents nowadays are more inclined to prefer iPad and television to teach their children. They believe that iPad teaches their kids better than books. Videos allow kids to see what the rhyme or story is telling. Kids do not have to use their minds much to learn the rhyme or poem, but as they grow, such activities will hamper the child's imagination. Parents are happy when their kids change the channel on YouTube. Parents exclaim, "He knows what to watch. He changes the channel by himself. He is so smart."

Nowadays, parents worldwide have stopped telling stories or reading stories to their children. They simply buy an iPad and give it to their kids from the age of 6 months and stay away from the headache, as they feel, of story-telling. But many researchers have confirmed that telling stories to children or reading stories on their own has positive benefits in brain development and the enhancement of imagination. According to a research paper published in 2019 on 'Stories and brain development: Reading aloud versus viewing videos,' reading stories with pictures connects the language centers and the centers for pictorial imagining in the children's brain more functionally than when watching a video. "The paper concluded that the reading of picture books in childhood promotes a person's creativity and viewing videos harm him (Thieme et al., 2019)." When a child watches a video, he is confined with a boundary of imagination; he cannot imagine beyond the creativity of the video. Whereas, in reading, a child can connect his imagination with the word and images he sees in the book. Thus, he has an infinite boundary of imagination. Reading, on the other hand, enhances the vocabulary power of children as well.

If someone wants to change his life but does not have any mentor, then the book of his choice can show him the right way. If we have a habit of reading, we would rather spend our time reading than hanging out with bad company. So, books can be our friends. In spirituality, we often believe that a day spent without reading a sentence is not well spent. We should try to read a book in a week. If not possible, read at least a paragraph a day. If you do not have time for even one paragraph, read at least a sentence every day. Reading has been emphasized in every culture throughout history.

There are basically two different genera of books; fiction and non-fiction. Fiction books are the primary sources of entertainment. When there was no internet and social media, people used to get entertained through novels. People either had to see live plays or read books for entertainment. Books were popular because it was the sign of being literate and educated. People would carry books just to look like a scholar. With the help of the fictional book, a person could take the source of entertainment wherever he desired. Because of books, the plays and dramas were not only limited to the auditorium only. Fictional books also enhance the imagination of a person. Moreover, it helps in building vocabulary. I personally like to read non-fiction more.

A child is very imaginative until he is introduced to the real world, the real struggle for existence. Maturity does not come with time; it is the byproduct of situations that life offers to everyone. So, there is no proper age limit where the imagination of a child ends. From age 8 to 14, I experienced being the most imaginative part of my life. According to a research paper published March 15th, 2021, on 'Brain development from newborn to adolescence: Evaluation by neurite orientation dispersion and density imaging' by Zhao Xueying and the team, the brain develops rapidly from birth to 2. After 2, the development of brains slows down. The total growth in the white matter was higher than that of the grey matter in the subjects of age 0-14 (Wei et al., 2021). Grey matter contains dendrites, unmyelinated axons, glial cells, and some capillaries.

This is responsible for higher brain functions such as memory, learning, self-control, decision-making, etc. On the other hand, white matter is responsible for establishing coordination between the brain and the spinal cord. Thus, after the age of 14, the development of grey matter slows down dramatically. As a result, we will have a hard time learning new skills and memorizing things. Because of this reason, it was easy for me to learn new things when I was between the ages 8 and 14.

Also, during that initial adolescence period, we are in the phase of physical and mental change. Our mind is working to prepare us for the real world. As the brain is so young, our mind can store much data without overwriting. As a result, our memory and imagination were at a high level. Wise parents realize this secret and try to shape their kids as they want because, at this age, all children are malleable in nature. All the information provided to kids will be absorbed faster. The slot of their subconscious mind is open for a longer time, and their conscious mind has no knowledge and power of the argument. This is why we say our childhood suffering can cause evil thoughts in our adulthood or in old age. The incidents those are saved in the sub-conscious mind as experiences have last long effects in our life. This is why all parents are advised not to act violently in front of any child. Any type of behavior a child establishes in that age group stays longer. The age between 6 to 14 is the perfect period of life to read fiction as much as a person can. This would help a child to advance and expedite his imagination power. Stories and comics that teach a good lesson should be read at the beginning of the age group, i.e., 6-10 years. When a child develops a habit of reading, he should be motivated to read novels. Reading novels should be slowed down now, and from the age of 15, a person should start picking non-fiction books. Non-fiction books related to money, the physical world, science, history, and life should be read. After the age of 15, a person should try to seek knowledge everywhere. The brain is expanding slower than before, and the sub-conscious level is well protected by the conscious mind. By the age of 25, the brain goes in the reverse direction; it degrades slowly. Thus, a person has to read and learn more about real-life from age 15 to 20. Nowadays, we have Facebook, Tik Tok, Instagram, movie theater, Twitter, Netflix, YouTube, Google, Hulu, and so many modes of entertainment. Reading is for knowledge, do not make it another source of entertainment; It used to be a long time ago when the world was not advanced. Minimize reading novels unless you are a novel writer. If you need entertainment, watch videos, make videos or do anything else.

Do not overload your brain, making it believe that you accomplished your reading quota by reading a novel. The novel is more for fun. After that entertainment break, read some non-fiction. You already learned to be imaginative; now it is time to learn something real and gain some skills. If you are trying to be a writer, a novelist, reading a novel is beneficial. However, you still need to read non-fiction books such as how to book. It is right that we can learn so much from a character of novels, but fictional characters are highly influenced by imagination. The reality you are facing will be far different from the plots of those novels. At the age of 15-20, you should be focusing on your career. Besides the studies of school, you need to find out your actual field of interest. Read about business or politics, as your wish but be practical and chose non-fictions. If you were never interested in reading a book before you were a teenager, the world has not ended yet. Later is always better than never. Start reading as much as you can.

At my early age, 5-8, I was enticed with poetry and stories. The first book I read was the famous literature of Nepal called 'Muna-Madan.' I still remember several lines of it. I was so much influenced by the book that I started composing poems. By the age of 14, I composed more than 2000 poems in three different languages and won several competitions. I finished writing manuscripts of 16 books by the age of 14; one was published in 2005-6, SPANDAN. I read many magazines and novels between the age of 8-14. They made me so imaginative that I could compose poems, songs, and stories wherever

I want. I never liked non-fiction books when I was a kid. I learned music especially, guitar and flutes. From the age of 14, I got interested in non-fictional books. I used to sleep with books. One side of my bed was literally occupied with well-stacked books that I would read before bed every day. Non-fiction books such as the power of your subconscious mind, how to win friends and influence people, and on music scripts, spiritual books, and so on.

Though I grew up in adversity, I never let any negativities of my surroundings influence me. Those books helped me to stick with the right paths. When I was a teenager, almost all my childhood friends fell into bad habits, drugs, and marijuana. I kept myself away from all those. I never drank, smoked, or committed any malicious activities. I was looking different and becoming different. By 20, I was well prepared for any kind of failure, misfortune, wretchedness, and misery; I could sustain any physical and mental stress. There was always some crisis going on in the family. There was no peace at all, but my reading habit motivated me to do something good all the time. I got addicted to reading. I started reading non-fiction books on different sorts of knowledge, such as reading body language, astrology, numerology, physics research paper, biography, science, VEDAS, the bible, etc. Reading provides knowledge and wisdom and gives motivation when you do not see hope, and there is no one for you.

When we read fictional books, stories, and novels, our brain goes to an Alpha level where the mind's capability of distinguishing real over fake is slightly diminished. We cannot enjoy novels if we read in conscious level, Beta waves. When we are totally consumed with the book, we can reach even more profound to theta level. We get excited and emotional with the flow of the story. If you are in a beta state, the protagonist's death does not matter because you know that it is just a story, but your mind lost the differences between reality and fiction in the alpha state or other upper levels. In such a case, your subconscious mind absorbs information faster. If we read a novel about violence and killing or suffering, our subconscious mind has the chance to record such details more. When some data is recorded on a subconscious level, it will convert into reality for sure. If you establish a habit of reading crime and murder, your brain will create low energy waves. You will have a hard time making a good relationship with people with a higher energy level. As we know, we are what we eat. Similarly, our mind is what we read. If you read fictional books, pick something that teaches you or motivates you for your goal.

On the other hand, non-fictional books can be boring to read because it is tough to get into Alpha level while reading these categories of books. You need your full awareness to learn anything, and when you are so aware, the conscious mind is very active. The information will still pass through your conscious mind while reading non-fiction. In this case, the conscious mind believes the authority and credibility of authors. It will not argue much and won't stop the information from reaching the subconscious level. Now, all good information is getting our inner level of mind, and when it is continued for a long time, our thinking pattern will be amazingly auspicious. We will be positive all the time. Our brain starts releasing the best level of energy, and our inner vibration will become stronger. We will be able to see opportunity in misfortune. Sooner or later, an optimistic person achieves his desired goals. It is believed that if a person reads more than 1000 books of the same categories, fiction or non-fiction, he will be able to guess the summary of the book just by reading its title and holding it on hand. I have felt this personally in my life. This is how I was able to finish reading 133 books in 6 months. I do not know how to explain this experience, but if you try yourself, you will understand more. In self-help books, let's talk about how to be rich kind of books, all authors talk about the exact same thing but in their own ways.

When you read many books about money, you will notice that the same information is written in all books. If you read about business, the essential data will be the same in all books. Thus, after reading 1000 books, you will become a fast reader. I often know the books' context without going through the books just by simply reading the title.

Sometimes, I doubt my intuition and read the entire chapter, then I realize that my inner feeling was right about the book. To be able to guess about the content of the book is possible only in non-fiction books. The writing style is straightforward; no beating around the bush. The sentences do not require to be flowery or overly creative. In fiction, everything is different. A beginner reader cannot complete a whole novel without an English dictionary on the side. Authors also try to make it almost impossible to grasp the connotation of the paragraph. I have found fictional books handy for SAT, GRE, and critical reading, but life starts after those tests. Therefore, focusing on non-fiction books would boost our motivation and understanding required for fighting real life out of the imaginative world. If you want to see the difference in readers' behavior, go hang out with novel lovers and non-fiction lovers. You will definitely find some vast differences, and then you will start reading non-fiction.

Summary Of Chapter IX

Reading can lead us to the subconscious level. The information we feed to our minds while reading has to be scrutinized. We are living in the era of entertainment; there are uncountable sources for fun. We must realize and use the books for their purpose, and the pursuit of books is to enlighten us, not to entertain us, at least today. In the past, we did not have Internet. Books were the only sources of fun, and people did not have choices but novels and stories. Reading novels has its own benefits, but we should realize the urgency of the time, and the time demands us to be more practical. If you do not prefer the Internet as a source of entertainment, then, of course, go for novels and stories for fun. But you still have to read non-fiction books; reading for enjoyment does not complete your reading task. If you extremely hate reading, there is an alternative: you have to hang around with some authors, businessmen, entrepreneurs, noble and optimistic people. If you are not vibrating in a particular wave and frequency, those intellectual personalities will make a distance from you because only the people of the same vibration stick around for long. Until you start vibrating at a better frequency, you will either be alone or in the wrong company. You can watch videos to motivate yourself, but as I already proved above, reading books has more benefits to our brain than watching a video.

Just read one or two paragraphs every day. Research about the best-selling books on non-fiction; read one of your choices every night before bed. If the knowledge of the book is practical, practice it every day and examine the effects. Once you build a habit of reading, your creativity and problem-solving capacity develop. Non-fiction books are the products of long research or self-experienced method. We can learn something in two hours that took a lifetime for authors to experience. To know the outcome of a study and experiment, we all need not conduct the same investigation again or do not need to bother traveling anywhere to learn some skills. Books do the same thing and also save our time, effort, and money.

Whether you chose to dive into spirituality or into a materialistic world, non-fiction books will help you enhance your energy level, making you ready for the further journey.

1. **Wake-up: 6 A.M.**
2. **Drink water, sip by sip.**
3. **Write dream tracking journal.**
4. **Drink the boiled water with my recipe.**
5. **Practice deep breathing in an open area.**
6. **Chant the mantra you created.**
7. **Physical exercise, flexibility, and Chess game**
8. **Practice visualization (does not have to be in the morning).**
9. **Be kind, and practice the willpower in as many activities as possible.**
10. **Eat healthy and detach yourself from unnecessary desires.**
11. **Exercises to find the reason of your existence.**
12. **Change your attitude towards the money.**
13. **Be courageous**
14. **Read a paragraph every day; non-fiction books**
15. **Self-hypnosis before bed/anytime.**
16. **Chant the mantra you created before bed.**

CHAPTER X

LEARNING A NEW SKILL

"Live as if you were to die tomorrow. Learn as if you were to live forever."- Mahatma Gandhi

Whether we notice or not, we learn something every day. We do not realize any minor activities that we know every day until it becomes a habit. From brushing our teeth to going to bed at night, we do many things; we meet many people and learn at least a few new skills or activities. However, those minor skills may, of course, drain the energy out of you but would not be powerful enough to change your life. In this competitive world, people are recognized because of their intellect and the skills they possess. We should master one skill or learn many of them; it is still debatable. The development of our brain slows down after the age of mid-20s. As I mentioned earlier in the previous chapter, the development of grey matter slows down significantly after 14. When the grey matter is not developing anymore, there will be more difficulty learning as we grow older.

Brain at the beginning of teen:

When we are at the beginning of teenage, our average weight of the brain reaches about 3 pounds, allowing us to think and compare several aspects and concepts at once. During that time, our frontal lobes can perform multiple tasks at once without any confusion.

Brain at the 20s:

When we reach the 20s, the development of the brain will be fully completed. The total growth of grey matter and white matter is almost finished. The knowledge and experiences acquired between the age of 8-14 determine the development of grey and white matter of the brain, and those activities performed at such age guide behaviors of a person and establish his habits. Based on intellect and experiences from an early age, a person will continue judgment, planning, and decision-making. That information he learned at an early age become a fundamental source of the intellect for him.

Brain at the 30s

As we grow older and hit the mid-30s, the number of neurons in the brain decreases. As a result, we start forgetting things and will take longer to learn new things. Memory power will degrade rapidly.

Brain at the 40s

According to research in the British Medical Journal, adults aged 40-50 suffer a declination of reasoning skill by 3.6% over 10 years; in every ten years, their reasoning capability is diminished by the given percentage. From the age of 40s, a person's memory starts depreciating, and the person will have difficulty memorizing the face of people and other complex information. I am saying the memory power starts decreasing but not suddenly becomes zero. A research paper published on April 1st, 2019, on 'Aging and recognition memory: a meta-analysis' by Aaron S. Benjamin and the team concludes that the recognition memory in an older adult generally declines dramatically than that of the young adult. They said, "There was also some evidence that older adults were particularly disadvantaged at remembering negatively valence-stimuli (except faces)." This means, older people tend to remember positive images and information more than negative ones, and it continues until the age of 80.

Brain at the 50s-60s

During this phase, the size of the brain starts shrinking. The elasticity of grey matter will be nominal. The brain is too overwritten. As a result, adding some skills and knowledge at this age will be difficult.

Brain at the 70s and above

At this age, a person is more likely to suffer from Alzheimer's or increase its risk by 80%. The blood flow in the brain cell will be less, and the chances of the build-up of deposits in the hippocampus are high. Hippocampus is responsible for forming new memories, and if there is build-up deposited, no new brain cells related to memories will be created. The brain receives a significantly less amount of oxygen from the body and generates comparatively less power. Since the brain's performance is decreased, a person's senses will stop work or become weak.

The development of the brain and other parts of the body is exactly how the older it gets, the more wear and tear it occurs. Our metabolism, physical strength, and brain size are at the peak of development when we are in teenage. As we grow older, everything slows down. Physical exercises have a direct impact on our body and brain. When we run, jog or walk and have deep breaths, our brain gets more oxygen, and there will be more blood flow. This can help our body to repair the impaired brain cell and strengthen our memory. A research journal published in April 2019 on 'Exercise and Hippocampal memory system' by Michelle W. Voss and the team confirms that an aerobic exercise such as dancing, swimming, cycling, football, soccer, etc., at least 150 min per week is good enough to strengthen our memory. While talking about weight lifting and resistance training (RT), the evidence suggests RT could boost but not replace the effects of aerobic exercise on memory (Voss et al., 2019).

Learning a new skill, no matter what age, requires the activity in grey matters. When we learn constantly, our brain continuously establishes relationships amongst neurons; neurons are the essential part of the communication system of our brain. Is it possible to strengthen our weak neurons or regrow them again? According to a journal article published in May 1998 in the Journal of College Science Teaching Vol. 27, No. 6, p.376, monkeys are constantly making new brain cells in the hippocampus, the area of the brain used for long term memory. The study was led by Dr. Elizabeth Gould at Princeton University. The article says, "The experts fully expect that humans are no different and that they make new brain cells in adult life." Still, there is no evidence of human neurons found in the spinal cord and the brain replicating themselves or regenerating themselves. However, the neurons (fibers) of the peripheral nerve that has been crushed or partly cut may slowly regenerate if the cell body is not thoroughly damaged. For now, only the thing we can do to promote the good health of neurons is following the use or lose principle; keep learning new skills that compel our neurons to perform their function. When there is enough mental and physical activity, neurons will get enough blood, oxygen, and energy that keep themselves healthy and young. On July 1st, 2014, a journal paper was published on 'Why exercise is good for your brain' by Katrin Weigmann. The article says, "It is found that the effect of learning is to keep cells alive. It is not making more cells, but it is making them survive." Learning a new skill like playing chess, dancing, playing musical instruments, and reading keeps our brain cells alive and prevents dementia (Weigmann, 2014).

When you are constantly learning something, you are using each cell regularly. This persistent activity in the cells makes them more flexible and younger for a long time. Some of the skills worthwhile to learn are:

Music Instruments

Everything around us, including ourselves, make a continuous sound as we all are vibrating. The human ear cannot perceive such low frequencies. By default, we rejoice with the melody that is soothing to us. Not everyone likes all genera of music, but we all want the natural sound of river, stream, and the wind blowing the leaves in the forest. Some sounds just touch our soul, and we feel liberated because that is the vibration of our inner mind. Our brain tries to mimic the sound frequency; we get overwhelmed with despondency when listening to sad songs. We feel good, bad, sad, or motivated depending upon the type of music we listen to. Listening to music, moreover, playing instruments, leads us to our subconscious level where we feel great.

According to a research paper published on May 1st, 2018, on 'The effect of music on Human Brain; frequency domain and time series analysis using electroencephalogram' by Rab Nawaz and the team, soothing music is found to take a listener into the upper Alpha state. This state of mind is very close to the subconscious mind. The experiment was conducted between two groups; one listening to soothing sounds and listening to the listener's favorite music. The team said, "In contrast to favorite music, relaxing music has a more soothing effect on the human brain in terms of increase in alpha power and reduced complexity. It is concluded that relaxing music composed of alpha binaural beats help acquire more relaxation than the listener's favorite music." Another research paper published on October 10th, 2013 on 'The effects of music on functional brain networks: a network analysis' by J. Wu and the team also confirmed that listening to music (playing instruments) releases the upper Alpha brain waves. This state of mind can cure us of physical afflictions. This is why people say music can cure illness. When I was in teen, I suffered from sinus, and it was so terrible that I often had a migraine and severe headache. Every time I had a migraine, I used to play guitar and sing for minutes. After singing 4 or 5 songs, the pain would go away. I do not know if it was a placebo effect, but I was getting better. That worked for me not one or two times, maybe a hundred times, and I still play instruments like flutes, piano, guitar, and violin when I get sick. I personally avoid drugs; even painkillers and music instruments become my pain killer in most cases. In my case, every time I played instruments, I give a job to my subconscious mind to cure me and to provide energy to my mind and body.

1. **Flute:** I play the classical bamboo flute that I learned sincc I was 8. When I am in a meditative state but not in the mood for meditation (at a random time), I take the flute of bass E or D scale, 2.5 and 3 feet long, which produces a longer wavelength. The sound coming out of these bass scales will have a lower frequency causing a lower pitch. This will be soothing to listen to. Since our mind tries to mimic the frequency of the flute, it produces a lower frequency brain wave. The chances of getting into the subconscious level are higher. If you decide to learn to play the flute, learn with the normal-sized bamboo flutes. I found this instrument more effective than others in the case of meditation. Flute requires a constant blow to produce sound. This will make you focus on breathing. When you practice sustaining notes for longer, your brain gets involved in the concentration exercise; you automatically concentrate on breathing. While learning this instrument, you are introducing a new skill to neurons and practicing mindfulness simultaneously.

2. **Guitar:** If you have never played it before, this may consume your entire energy of the day. You really need to have a strong reason behind learning guitar. Otherwise, you will simply quit learning after a few days or weeks. Learning guitar is different from learning flute or piano. Strings will give you a terrible experience that will stop you from learning it, or at least, you will be highly discouraged by the pain. My brother borrowed a guitar for two nights from a friend when I was 12. It was festival time, so he got busy with other stuff, but I tried learning

it the whole night. I learned 7 'major' chords in one night. The next day, the fingertips of the left hand were swollen and filled with water. I continued learning minor chords because, after that day, the guitar would be gone. Fortunately, we got to keep the guitar for one more week. That was the week when I learned all 'minor' and 'major' chords. By the end of the week, I was able to play in songs; not perfect but just alright. I played in the Deepawali night, a street concert of my town next week. All of my friends were surprised to see me learning guitar that quick; in one week. I never took classes or anything formal pieces of training. I played in several local concerts in festivals, schools, colleges, and universities in the US. I usually play guitar when I am feeling low and energy less. The sound of strings makes me feel connected with my soul and helps me to eliminate all of the agonies my body goes through.

3. **Piano:** I love this instrument because it helps me activate both hemispheres of my brain. You have to use both hands to play and produce bass, chords, and fingering notes. You will learn coordination between two hands. As a result, your non-dominant hand will come into use. The exercise of your non-dominant hand will put extra effort on the neurons that have not been fully used for long. There will be enough blood flow, and the internal communication among neurons gets stronger. This will eventually help in boosting up the memory. On the other hand, the appeasing sound of the piano will take you to the upper Alpha state. The pain level on this instrument will be moderate unless you have a corporal tunnel issue or arthritis problem.

Painting

Many types of research have been done on art therapy, and it is found that art and painting support mental health. When we cannot express our experiences in words, arts play a vital role in doing so. In the time of stress, if you start painting or sketching, the stress level will be diminished. This is one of the most exciting skills to add to one's life. While painting, you will be fully absorbed in it. As a result, you will be away from stress. On the other hand, as you progress in learning, satisfaction will take you to a different mind state. I had a student I taught some basic sketching skills, smudging, and fundamentals of light and shade of colors. He practiced every day and created some fantastic paintings from his imagination. Learn painting and try to draw what you see in your mind. This will help you to identify the activities of your thoughts. If you are inclined to create many negative-vibe pictures, such as images of killing and crimes, you can guess that your subconscious mind has been fed negative information more. Since the subconscious mind understands pictures more than words, you can divert your interest and draw more positive paintings. The more you focus on painting auspicious things, the more impressive your life will be. Painting is another crucial skill that can lead you towards the subconscious level easily. I started drawing at the same time when I began learning flutes.

Dancing

Learning dance is not only a physical thing but also a mental exercise. This is one of the weakest parts of my life. I always try to avoid dancing. However, I tried learning it and participated in the school and university dancing show a few times. Now, I do it for exercise purposes only; I never learned with dedication. Every time I have tried learning, it has given me the psychological boost to erase the fear of inferiority I have in my mind. In my second deployment in 2019, my boss- chief always motivated me to attend SALSA night. I always made excuses because I was too shy to dance with beautiful ladies, especially when I do not know the dancing. Finally, one day I was convinced and attended a session; it was fun. I remember that I was the only one who was sweating too much while learning. I overcame my shyness. Dancing is the best activity that activates our neurons and keeps them alive. Dancing was the best skill to learn to prevent dementia, as mentioned earlier in the research paper published by Katrin Weigmann.

Singing

I sing for fun but not to perform because my voice is not trained or good enough for the stage. Singing can be a reasonable means of meditation. When I play guitar and sing 3 or 4 songs, it cures my physical and mental sufferings. Singing also means producing vibrations. If we focus on our tone and create a low frequency with a longer wavelength, it gives a soothing sound. Our whole body vibrates with a gentle frequency. Singing can lead us to the upper Alpha stage easily.

New Language

As we get older, we find difficulty learning new languages because we will not memorize new words effectively; the connection between neurons gets weaker in older cells. But if we force ourselves, nothing is impossible. In 2017, I was in Baghdad, the US army base. People working in the laundry were native Arabic speakers. I decided to learn the language and started working on it. I memorized almost 50 sentences within a week and could communicate for 3-5 minutes without an accent. I had a Nepali, Hindi, and Urdu background. Thus, the pronunciation was not a big issue for me to learn Arabic. However, my intention was not to learn the language; my plan was to use time and use my brain to learn something new.

I read somewhere that learning a new language or any new skills helps us grow more dendrites out of our neurons in the brain. The main functions of dendrites are to receive signals from other neurons, process the signals received, and transfer the information to the neuron's soma. Soma is the cell body where the signals from the dendrites are joined and passed on. So, scientifically, learning a new language or anything basically helps our brain to communicate better. Thus, I was using the opportunity that Army provided me in learning the language. One day, I went to the laundry to pick up my clothes. There were few soldiers ahead of me picking up their clothes. I started talking to the laundry personnel in Arabic. I was in uniform. Other soldiers looked at me and got confused because they thought I was speaking excellent Arabic. When I was leaving from there, a voice from behind said, "How was your day, soldier?" I turned around to find that the person was a lieutenant colonel. We talked all the way to his office. He was pretty impressed with my Arabic, and he thought I was of Arab descendent. When I told him that I have been learning the language for a week, he was surprised. At that time, I was in my late 20s. I was supposed to forget things at this age, and the number of neurons was supposed to go down, as science says. I learned a new language at the same speed that I used to learn anything when I was in my teenage.

Memorizing Maps

This is an excellent exercise to practice. Try to draw a map of your neighborhood. See if you can remember all the small details. Try to make stop signs and write the street names. When you are done, compare it with the actual google map. It is found that a person who is good at memorizing the map or the street or who can travel places without the help of GPS, his brain cells are working perfectly. Moreover, the cells are getting younger, and the number of dying neurons as he gets older is less.

Summary Of Chapter X

Every time we learn something new, more dendrites grow out of neurons. These dendrites are responsible for the communication among the neurons via brain signals. When there is an adequate flow of signals, the brain works properly. If signals are blocked and not passed in or out to the soma, we lose the connection among neurons. As a result, neighboring neurons do not get the information that leads to memory loss. To sharpen the memory and enhance the creativity level of the brain, we should keep on learning every day. You can learn the same thing over and over to get better at it, or you can try a new something every day. If you want to be master of one, it is good but becoming a jack of all is not bad either. Nobody is perfect, and you cannot learn something in perfection; there is always room for improvement. You do not have to make a specific timetable to practice this. Just try to learn something from everyone you meet every day. If our brain is weak, then our whole body is feeble. A small ignorable activity can bring a significant change in our minds and body. If you want your brain to be younger or aging slower, you should follow my advice today; learn something new every day.

1. **Wake-up: 6 A.M.**
2. **Drink water, sip by sip.**
3. **Write dream tracking journal.**
4. **Drink the boiled water with my recipe.**
5. **Practice deep breathing in an open area.**
6. **Chant the mantra you created.**
7. **Physical exercise, flexibility, and Chess game**
8. **Practice visualization (does not have to be in the morning).**
9. **Be kind, and practice the willpower in as many activities as possible.**
10. **Eat healthy and detach yourself from unnecessary desires.**
11. **Exercises to find the reason of your existence.**
12. **Change your attitude towards the money.**
13. **Be courageous**
14. **Read a paragraph every day; non-fiction books**
15. **Self-hypnosis before bed/anytime.**
16. **Chant the mantra you created before bed.**
17. **Learn something new every day.**

CHAPTER XI

IMPORTANCE OF BEING ALONE

"No one saves us but ourselves. No one can and no one may. We ourselves must walk the path."- Gautama Buddha

Who is your best friend? Friends are the most vital element of our life. As we are social animals, we cannot live alone for long. We have so many things going on in our lives, and we need someone to share our stories. When we have hard times in our lives and cannot be shared with family, we share them with our friends. Sometimes the relationship of emotions is better than that of the blood. Friends have a more significant impact on our life; we become how our friends are. Either we become as our friends are, or they become like us; somebody changes. Generally, a person's character is we always tend to mold other people into their own way. Everybody likes others to behave like them. When we meet someone new, we try to influence them with our skills and qualities. We want people to follow our advice.

We become happy when our friends do what we suggest. Especially when two persons get married, they create a mental boundary for each other, a list of rules. When one crosses the border, the other gets mad. Sometimes, the process of constructing boundaries in their mind ends the relationship. In most cases, one dominates the other, and even they make decisions for one another.

One will decide what others will pursue in life as a career. So many compromises will happen in marriages, yet the life partner is the best friend one can have in his life. Besides life partners, other friends play a crucial role in our life.

When you meet someone adorable and exciting, you wish to see them again. If you like them for some reason, you love to be around them. But if we misunderstand them and when our ego clashes with somebody else, we never want to see them again in our lives. This is human nature. While trying to appease ourselves, we tend to be friends of good and bad people. Also, we indulge ourselves in so many materials to divert our minds from the real issues. We try to find friends and family to listen to our problems. They may be available once, twice, or thrice. One day, they will be tired of us. Even your life partner will hesitate to hear you when you complain much and cannot solve anything independently. Finally, when you do not find anyone to take part in your despondency, spend a few seconds in the dark and ask yourself, "Who is your best friend?"

Most people never realized that a person's best friend is himself. Now, you may ask me that 'you' and 'yourself' are the same person. How can I be my own friend? This sounds to be a philosophical matter. In the actual case, you are the unhappy one and seeking a friend to share your feelings. 'You' defines the external connection of your mind in my definition above. 'Yourself' is that personality you have never been introduced to; you never wanted to know that person within you. When you have problems, you went to your parents or friends to get advice. But nobody can be with you 24/7 except 'yourself.' How is your relationship with yourself? If you want to find it out, follow the instruction as follows. Find a peaceful place in your house. Tell everyone not to disturb you for the next two hours. Take your cell phone with you, fine for this exercise. Set up the alarm 2 hours from now. Once the alarm is set up, do not touch the phone again for two hours. Turn off the light. The darker the room is, the better the effect. Now, just sit on a chair, floor, or bed and do nothing. Do not even try meditation; simply do nothing. Can you survive 2 hours effortlessly? How is your feeling? If you touched a cell phone once or twice only, it is not bad, but if you picked it several times, you need to be careful. What were other activities you did when you were supposed to do nothing? Be honest with yourself. See, even in this sentence- be honest to yourself, 'you' is being suggested, to be honest to 'yourself.' If you find many distracting activities such as laying on the bed, singing, dancing, writing, reading, babbling, or anything that makes you busy during the exercises, you are trying to avoid or ignore yourself. How you ignore the presence of a person you do not like? By doing the activities I just mentioned, right? If you were allowed to go outside the room before the alarm goes off, you would definitely rush out. How would you react if there was a lady of your dream in the room? Two hours would feel like 5 minutes for you this time, isn't it? Einstein is very correct; the time is relative.

The problem with people nowadays is they do not like their own company. If they are left alone for some time, they start getting frustrated. If the loneliness prolongs, they get depressed and commit suicide. The physical body, which I termed 'you' in the example, will hate the inner mind, which I termed 'yourself.' Inner mind provokes the physical body by thoughts. When the physical body dislikes the thoughts and the feelings coming out from the inner self, it tries to find another physical friend, social media, entertainment, family, and friends, to get distracted. The physical body enjoys until it is with someone or something, but as soon as it gets alone, the similar thoughts and the feelings hunt him again. In such a battle of 'you' and 'yourself,' the loss for either side is the same. We spend our entire life finding friends, relatives, and the right life partners. Without connecting I with myself or you with yourself, all other outside connections are a waste.

There is always joy and happiness when there is a harmonious relationship between these two entities; you will have your best friend wherever you go. If you practice staying in the dark for a few minutes every day, you will be able to tolerate yourself very soon. You will start enjoying your own company. You might know some people who travel alone and does most things alone for fun. Actually, those people know the secret about real happiness. Instead of making hundreds of friends outside, they accept themselves as the friend they needed. Now, they do not have to call anyone to hang out or have no chance for anyone to hurt their feelings. When a person knows what is good for him from his inner heart and soul, he has less chance of suffering, physically and mentally. If your inner being is not happy, no matter what topic people argue, it always sounds bitter to you. You do not need anybody else to listen to your issues besides yourself. If there is only one person who cares for you the most is yourself, and if somebody knows you the most is yourself. If you reject this relationship, you will never be fulfilled.

Once you find out that you cannot stand yourself, the purpose of the exercise is done. You do not need to practice this unless you want to. It has really a significant impact on our life if you practice it every day. 'Doing absolutely nothing is a yogic way to establish a good relationship with our mind and body where each and all cells of our body get relaxed. There are so many other positive byproducts of this solitude exercise. For example:

Activation Of Upper Alpha Level

When you practice solitude for 10 to 15 minutes a day in the dark, your entire body will be in a deeply relaxed state if you accomplished the exercise very well. Since your mind is not so active with external materials, it starts looking for something inside to get occupied. If you do this exercise in a happy mood, you are more likely to get benefited more. You may feel lightness or some other sensations in your spine or head. Do not even try to control your thoughts; just do nothing. Watch your thoughts if they bother you much. Do not hold onto any emotions. Slowly, your mind gets less information to process and gets more relaxed. Because of the deep relaxation, your brain starts releasing upper Alpha waves. This does not happen overnight but indeed happens one day.

1. Build self-control: When we face several hardships in our life, most of the problems might have arisen from within ourselves. The practice of solitude will help us to locate the real cause of the issues. By eliminating a problem from its root, we will get rid of the issue forever from our life. We will be able to see our weaknesses. Most of us act stupid when we are mad and when we are driven by our ego. This solitude exercise helps us to see the ego and control our emotions.

2. Self-respect: After establishing an excellent relationship with your mind, you will not need any assistance from other persons to make a proper decision in your life. You will understand your responsibility. This will build your self-esteem.

There are many more benefits that you will receive as the outcome of the exercise; you even do not have to think about them. However, to be alone and happy is extremely difficult. If you practice solitude in a good mood, all good consequences are inevitable.

Practicing Silence Fasting

This is a less popular form of fasting. A person does not eat or drink in regular fasting, but a person is mute for the day in silence fasting. Some people even make the practice harder by taking all gadgets away from them. They avoid phones, TV, radio, computer, or any sort of communication and entertainment. This is the moment of utter silence where no information is coming into the mind, and no energy is leaving the body in the form of sound waves. The first advantage is clear that fasting saves mental energy.

When someone is fasting and not eating and drinking, the digestive organs get rest, and the energy required to digest food can be diverted towards the brain. There will be less load on the brain to release several enzymes to digest food. Similarly, when a person is mute and not around any source of information, his mind will not get unnecessary information to process. The mind will swing around the thoughts that it had previously. You may desire to speak, but you cannot because of fasting. Thoughts are like the electrons running inside the wire. They are running inside your mind and trying to get out of it. When you connect with entertainment such as a phone or speaking to others, those thoughts flow out of you just like electrons flow out when connecting a light bulb or other electronic devices to the circuit. At least, electrons are moving with a purpose; what about your thoughts? Do they have any directions or motives? Our thoughts, when they flow out of our minds, need to have ambitions. They should not be wasted in vain. Neither should they run continuously in our minds. What happens when electrons run continuously on a conductor?

The result is evident that running electrons collide with the conductor's atoms, and the conductor gains kinetic energy, but it is not moving anywhere. I mean, some kinetic energy of each electron is transferred to the conductor's atoms, but the conductor is not moving. The kinetic energy will be transformed into thermal energy. In other words, the resistance of the conductor tries to stop the motion of the electrons. Thus, the wire or conductor gets hot. If the battery provides electrons, there will be an electric field on both sides of the battery or source. The flow of electrons is due to this electric field because the electric field pulls the electrons. Similarly, when thoughts are running in our minds, they stimulate neurons in the brain. Thoughts get transformed into electrical signals in the brain. Then the signals travel from one neuron to another with the help of dendrites. As a result, the brain creates a small electromagnetic field. The more the thoughts, the stronger the magnetic field. This greater electromagnetic field pulls or pushes the electrons in and out of the neurons continuously, and the overflow of signals in neurons can raise the thermal energy in dendrites. Of course, our body has a natural mechanism to cool them down. However, overheated dendrites may give us memory issues or may lead to difficulty in communication among neurons. If our dendrites were superconductors, I mean zero resistance of charge, the communication among neurons would be in the speed of light (I am saying very high speed) with no production of thermal energy in dendrites. We would have photo memory, and other functions of our brain such as recovering the wounds, replacing old cells, curing the diseases, and so on would be performed effortlessly. To achieve this phenomenon, some people believe in consuming gold little by little. When the atoms of gold start building up in their blood and eventually, in their neurons, they think to achieve such supernatural abilities in life. That is only the hypothesis and the subject of future research.

When we have too many thoughts, we have two best choices: 1st, to convert thoughts into actions, and 2nd, to hold them into the mind and keep watching them without reacting to them. We can simply talk and waste them in vain too. This is what we all usually do. Acting on every thought as the first choice suggests is nearly impossible but following the 2nd choice is practicable. When we do not react to the thoughts, we do not give them extra energy of emotions. With the lack of energy, thoughts become less effective in our neurons. The motion of the electric signals will be slower, causing more minor wear and tear of the neurons and dendrites. No need to react to any thoughts unless it is a life-changing idea; just keep watching them. Save the extra energy by muting yourself, and let the brain use that energy to repair your body. I used the example of electrons and conductors to understand the relation of thoughts and the dendrites; it is not there to compare an electric circuit with the brain.

You need to practice silence every day for a short period. Increase the time little by little, and then you can do it for a whole day. Staying silent does not mean doing nothing. A person can do a lot of things while being quiet. I want you to do nothing and remain silent. This is the hardest part. Thus, practice it for 10 min and increase the time as you like. Just practicing 10 min of silence will boost up your thinking power, and you feel refresh. When we are not talking for hours, our most prominent part of the brain, the cerebrum, will be less busy. Other body parts such as the motor cortex, cerebellum, arcuate fasciculus, vocal cord, Broca's area, tongue, and throat will get rest. Just by controlling one activity, we give a break to a lot of our body parts. When suddenly many parts take rest, there will be extra energy in the brain. That extra energy will be used to repair the torn part of your cells. Sometimes, people can heal another person via reiki or simply by his thoughts. This is a way to utilize the energy we get from the brain. Your brain will never be able to heal someone else until you are completely healed in and out. If you spend all your energy talking, working, and overthinking, you will always run out of energy. Stop your brain from overthinking and avoid over-talking. This will definitely help you to save mental energy.

If you practice silence every day, the life energy within you gets accumulated, and when it is too excessive, your aura will burst with ecstasy. Animals will be pleased to be around you. You will have so much life energy within you that your touch can eliminate the pain of people. Your entire cells will vibrate with a different level of blissfulness. But this is not achievable by one day or two days of practice. To get some reiki power, you must meditate for 10,000+ hours in your life. As I already mentioned, to heal someone, you need to be in perfect health. All energy you get from months of meditation is just adequate or less for yourself. Even if you are willing to cure someone, you cannot. Healing someone means passing on the life force from your body to the victim. Thus, do not be enticed with the reiki effect for now. Focus on the exercises mentioned above, practice these proven ways and see the changes yourself. You will find the difference.

Summary Of Chapter XI

People are afraid of themselves nowadays that they cannot spend little time alone. When the light and Internet are out, they act like the world is ending soon. Many people are connected to gadgets and entertainment so much that their life without such devices is meaningless. In case such devices are taken away from them, they will go crazy. Children nowadays are raised with these gadgets. If they are not happy with the entertainment provided on line, they want to go out and find people and friends to hang out with. A person constantly looks for someone to share his feelings with. When there is a tough time in life, people tend to get involved in the wrong companion because they like people who listen to them when they need listeners. They fall into an inappropriate relationship quick because they were trying to run away from something, could be mental or physical. In the quest of finding a perfect listener, a person establishes friendship and relationships with as many people as he can. When somebody seems to be caring, he trusts them. He tries everything possible to mitigate his sufferings. Eventually, sooner or later, he fails again. Instead of focusing on pleasing everyone, he should have focused on knowing his mind and becoming a friend of himself. You should be happy when the light goes off. You should feel amazing when the Internet is down because that is the time you can be with yourself. Do not go out for a walk or drive when the Internet is out. Instead, learn to be happy with yourself. When you are so glad alone, none can mess with your inner peace. You will never need anyone to listen to you; you are self-sufficient. When you are alone, you need to learn to save the energy that your brain uses to perform various functions of your body. Adding a practice of silence while you are alone can boost up the level of friendship between you and your thoughts.

A great deal of energy is used when we talk. If you are speaking in a foreign language, the amount of energy utilized is even high. Talking not only involves our vocal cord and tongue. There are many other brain parts involved in this activity. When we voluntarily give those organs rest, some amount of energy is saved. The excess amount of energy is now used in the repair of our worn and torn cells. This means, if we talk less, we get healed more. There is no way to stop thoughts suddenly. We just need to watch them but not react to them. Thoughts are like venomous snakes; do not mess with them; they will go away without hurting you.

1. **Wake-up: 6 A.M.**
2. **Drink water, sip by sip.**
3. **Write dream tracking journal.**
4. **Drink the boiled water with my recipe.**
5. **Practice deep breathing in an open area.**
6. **Chant the mantra you created.**
7. **Physical exercise, flexibility, and Chess game**
8. **Practice visualization (does not have to be in the morning).**
9. **Be kind, and practice the willpower in as many activities as possible.**
10. **Eat healthy and detach yourself from unnecessary desires.**
11. **Exercises to find the reason of your existence.**
12. **Change your attitude towards the money.**
13. **Be courageous**
14. **Read a paragraph every day; non-fiction books**
15. **Self-hypnosis before bed/anytime.**
16. **Chant the mantra you created before bed.**
17. **Learn something new every day.**
18. **Stay alone and practice silence for 10min every day.**

CHAPTER XII

WRITING

"The writer is an explorer. Every step is an advance into a new land."- Ralph Waldo Emerson

Writing is one of the many ways of introducing our ideas to the world. Similarly, it is the same route to feed all information to our inner consciousness. Writing, just like reading or speaking, uses several parts of our brain and body. When we read or write, Broca's Area and Wernicke's area gets activated. Their function is to turn the words and sentences into meanings. The frontal lobe and parietal lobe are responsible for judgment, movement, problem-solving and other essential functions involve in the writing. Writing helps us remember things more effectively because the physical act of writing will cause the information to move towards the forefront and then trigger our brain to pay close attention. As a result, we understand and memorize things for a long time.

When we write our thoughts on a piece of paper, our brain releases hormones, and many thoughts decrease. A research paper was published on 20th December 2017 on 'The healing properties of writing for persons with mental health conditions' by Kristine Lynn Haertl and Adrienne Maiers Ero-Phillips. The research found that the act of writing actually works as a therapeutic tool for patients. Their results demonstrated the importance of writing to enhance the understanding of the self and others and promote health and healing (Haertl et al., 2017). To heal our wounds or wear and tear the cells, our upper level of Alpha waves should be activated, but our conscious mind won't allow us to access its upper level if we are constantly thinking. While writing, the brain focuses on one activity; our active mind will be busy in the writing process. Once we start enjoying writing, we slowly move towards the subconscious level. As soon as we start vibrating in different frequencies, the excess amount of energy will be released, and that energy will be used to heal our worn area of the cells.

On the other hand, seeing is believing; when we write our wishes in detail, the chances of getting our desires to pass down to the subconscious level becomes high. Everything we are trying to do is taking control over our subconscious mind and getting ready for all possibilities that our life can be. Writing 100 words a day for 45 days can activate your unawaken neuron cells leading you to be more imaginative. You will begin to see the world from a different perspective; in fact, you will analyze things from various aspects and with several points of view. Some important writing exercises would be:

Freewriting

Set up a regular schedule for this exercise, usually in the morning or evening. Choose a place where no one will disturb you. You need to have pen and paper; typing is not as effective as writing on paper. Also, have your cellphone with you for the alarm set up. Set the alarm for 3 minutes and begin writing. You should not be thinking about any topic before you hit the alarm's start button. No subject is required. Just try to brainstorm. Write as much as you can. Do not overthink about the grammar or spelling; avoid overthinking. Just follow the thoughts and write down how they appear in your mind. Everything you see, feel, smell, sensation, or anything you observe in your mind, put them on the paper. The more you write in 3 minutes, the more you benefit. Stop writing after the alarm goes off. When you are done, read it aloud. How does it sound? Find out if it is an optimistic tone or a pessimistic one. Then scrutinize all the words. Count the total number of words in the paragraph. Find out the numbers of positive, negative, and neutral expressions. Neutral words help form a sentence but do not carry a positive or negative meaning such as a, an, the, in, sometimes, etc. Sometimes the negative words give a positive meaning. In such a case, count that negative word as a positive one. Then calculate the percentage of negative and positive out of total thoughts you had in 3 minutes. The following example is an excerpted from my book, ARKAINIST; A Boy from The Sun. I tried to show the calculation of negative and positive words and their percentage.

"It would be stupendous if everything, once existed, lingers forever in the universe. But, the principle of nature is harsh; things that came out of nothingness will return to void perishing all quiddities, and then, the entire multiverse will coalesce into a single point dissolving into the emptiness. In the beginning, there was nothing, and at the end, there will be nothing but just a sound: the sound of explosions because the universe is collapsing soon."

Total word count = 76

Positive meaning words = stupendous, everything, existed, lingers, forever, came out, beginning = 7

Negative meaning = But, harsh, nothingness, void, return, perishing, coalesce, dissolving, emptiness, nothing, nothing, explosions, collapsing = 13

Neutral meaning = 56

Negative % = 17.11%

Positive % = 9.21%

Neutral % = 73.68%

Total sentences = 6

Positive sentence = 1 = 16.67%

Negative sentence = 5 = 83.33%

If we look at everything in detail, there are more numbers of neutral words in the sentence. Negative words are almost as twice as much the positive ones. But if we look at the sentence, negative sentences are five times more than positive. So, after dissecting thoughts, we see that the meaning of individual words for our minds is confusing. Until the sentence is complete, we cannot determine the sense of it is positive or negative. Also, having too many helping words, neutral words can overcrowd the subconscious level. Therefore, writing a wish in 3 positive words can help your subconscious level perform with more accuracy.

In this example, while writing the paragraph, my mind was vibrating in a negative energy zone. Thankfully, this paragraph is from my Novel book, not from my own life experience. This was just an ordinary passage example when I had a topic to write on. I forced myself to vibrate with such a pessimistic level to bring the feeling of pessimism.

Count your words and find out if there are many negative sentences. Do not try to avoid any negative comments because you need to see them fix your thought patterns. When you know you have many negative feelings about your writing, find out what it is about. Is it about your economic life, love life, or spiritual life? Once you guess the cause of your feelings of the day, write it with a big size letter and move on. Keep on doing this for 7 days. After a week, check the pattern of your feelings if the causes of emotions are changed. If the reason for your sadness is the same or somewhat similar, then fix it or forget it. If the solution is on your hand, such as working an extra shift to pay off your car loan, do it. If your girlfriend married somebody else, then forget her.

Summary Of Chapter XII

Observing thoughts in the mind is very difficult, and it requires exercises for a long time to see thoughts and separate them from ourselves. When you close your eyes, you may realize some thoughts crossing your mind. You will follow it but suddenly get entangled in the web of thoughts. It is not that easy to find the root cause of thoughts by watching in mind; it is distracting. Instead, for beginners, writing down thoughts under time pressure is more beneficial. When the clock clicks, the pressure builds up, and the conscious mind gets nervous to accomplish the task. It requires the assistance of the subconscious level to finish the job in time. When the door of the subconscious level is opened, all feelings hidden in the brain waiting to turn into reality will try to flow out on the paper. The conscious mind will still filter most of them. However, something is better than nothing. When this is done daily, slowly but steadily, we will know what the mind was preparing to bring in reality. If it is a misfortune, we need to alter them. If it is an auspicious one, we will amplify them.

1. **Wake-up: 6 A.M.**
2. **Drink water, sip by sip.**
3. **Write dream tracking journal.**
4. **Drink the boiled water with my recipe.**
5. **Practice deep breathing in an open area.**
6. **Chant the mantra you created.**
7. **Physical exercise, flexibility, and Chess game**
8. **Practice visualization (does not have to be in the morning).**
9. **Be kind, and practice the willpower in as many activities as possible.**
10. **Eat healthy and detach yourself from unnecessary desires.**
11. **Exercises to find the reason of your existence.**
12. **Change your attitude towards the money.**
13. **Be courageous**
14. **Read a paragraph every day; non-fiction books**
15. **Self-hypnosis before bed/anytime.**
16. **Chant the mantra you created before bed.**
17. **Learn something new every day.**
18. **Stay alone and practice silence for 10min every day.**
19. **Free-writing 3 min a day.**

CHAPTER XIII

DISCIPLINE

"Discipline is the bridge between goals and accomplishment."
-Jim Rohn

Discipline is the quality of being able to continue doing a particular course of action in all conditions regardless of the interest and desire of the person. A person requires strong willpower to demonstrate an unshakable discipline in his life. Starting some activity or plan can be easy, and continuing it for a few days is even easier than commencing it, but performing the action for an extended period is back-breaking. Being able to decide and choose the must-done activities daily demands a great deal of self-control. When a person is disciplined, he ought to perform many actions that he might abhor a lot. If a person is more sensible and reasoning, he would definitely abide by self-control and be persistent in his actions. Discipline in a person is like a GPS in a car. The driver's destination is the motivator action for GPS; without a destination, GPS would not show any route, and without a proper way, a car and its passenger would not reach their destination.

Similarly, discipline cannot last long without a goal. I mean, if you just want to set up a discipline of waking up early with no purpose of it, you will not be able to push yourself harder for this habit. The goal is the driving force behind establishing a positive habit, and the habit is the building block of discipline. For example, to meet a goal, you wake up early every day; it becomes your habit. You perform all the actions required for the achievement of your target at a particular specific time. You may have to quit something or add some new activities to the list, but you are performing all actions diligently; now, you are disciplined.

Self-discipline sometimes seems to be self-punishing because you do most of the activities you do not like and separate from the stuff you want to do. When we try to discipline our kids or pets, the situations become the same; discipline becomes the punishment. This means, being discipline is very painful for you and people around you as well. It is so because being discipline is a process, and you have not seen the outcome yet, especially in kids and pets; they never know why they were told to do some actions. The reward of discipline may not be available to harvest every day, but it will undoubtedly turn into fruition one day. Patience is the quality that anchors discipline at its place. When there is no patience in a person to wait for some time to see if the seed he sowed is sprouting, he keeps digging out the seed off the soil. This only lowers the chances of growing the seed and eventually makes it defective. He needs patience. Likewise, when a person has a strong desire and goal to achieve, he sets up a particular discipline. If he loses patience, he will break his discipline, and when it is broken, his car will lose the directions to go to his destination to achieve his goal. Things are interrelated though they may look independent to each other. When one thing collapses, the other ceases too.

Discipline also requires some rules and regulations that a person should abide by. When there is a violation of personal limitations, he should punish himself so that discipline is not taken as a joke or a piece of cake. Rules are there for a reason. If you do not retaliate and correct yourself at the right time, you will make a habit of breaking the rules. As a result, instead of becoming a disciplined person, you would be a reckless one. After that, forget your goal and the success. You can exceed your limit only when you can overcome the hindrances and pains that come across on your way of discipline. If I violate any of my personal rules of discipline, I punish myself so that it would make me even better in the long run.

I remember an incident when I was performing a meditation, 'Bangla-Mukhi Sadhana,' which was the ritual of 21 days, and I missed the 20th day. The punishment was I had to fast every Monday for a month. I resumed the practice the next day, but that was not the last day of the sadhana. Actually, I started entire rituals over again. Thus, it was my first day of sadhana, even after finishing it for 19 days. This was another part of self-punishment. The ritual itself was painful; I had to wake up at 3:50 A.M., shower with cold water, start mantra rituals, eat once a day, self-made food cooked in a specific way, no napping during the day, no TV, and no female contacts at all. I was almost done with it but had to restart. I accomplished it in my second trial and achieved the outcome that I was looking for as the consequences of the sadhana. If there is no discipline in a person, sadhana is impossible for him. Sadhana is a complex form of meditation with specific rituals, rules, beliefs, disciplines, and understandings.

A person can meditate for no reason and may not be willing to achieve anything but a sadhak who meditates has a reason for his meditation, and he is firmly ready to fulfill his desires. Having desires is not always bad, but the kind of desires can be undesirable sometimes. Buddha had a passion for knowing things and acquiring knowledge. He did not leave the palace just for fun. He meditated for the fulfillment of his desire. Likewise, all sadhaks have some desires associated with their meditation practices, and they need a strict disciplinary lifestyle. Whatever you do, whether related to the materialistic world or spiritual world, you have to follow specific rules, and you are compelled to be bound with discipline or suffer.

Discipline makes the future almost predictable in the sense that if you are walking towards the East and there is a church on the way, then it is predictable that you might see the church. If you do not see it, that is a different case. Similarly, if you do some set of activities every day towards your goal, you are likely to see much more hindrances and pleasant outcomes on the way. You may be completely oblivious to those facts, but their effects will create a mark in your mind as experiences that would eventually help your character form a firm discipline. When you see some minor but instant benefits of being discipline, your willpower will boost up, and you will get the enthusiasm to carry on your activities. Thus, if you want to set up some disciplinary actions for yourself or others, do not make too strict at first. If you have never woke up at 6 A.M., do not assume to wake up at 3:50 A.M. tomorrow all of sudden. Before you come up with some rigid rules, you need to warm up with the similar but more flexible ones first, and then, you can construct an austere skeleton of regulations. Being discipline will take away your unnecessary freedom. I am saying unnecessary freedom to that freedom that allows you to smoke, drink, hang out with no purpose, excessive shopping, and other destructive habits. Discipline will give you a borderline that is not supposed to cross.

The limit and boundaries created by your rules have upcoming hidden secrets of your success. Once the goal is achieved, the discipline related to the respective purpose will vanish, just like when the car arrives at its destination, GPS will stop showing the further routes. If you decide to achieve something new or just add a few more goals in your life, such purposes demand a new discipline set. Some disciplines are suitable to be remained constant throughout life if possible, such as waking up early in the morning and eating more vegetables. Anyway, the ultimate goal of life is to live long, healthy, happy, and prosperous. We must have self-control in determining and choosing what is beneficial in the long run. If you want to go to the hospital which is at East, you cannot walk towards North and complain that there is no hospital. You walked; you definitely did your job, but it was all in vain because you did not have a proper direction. If you had a GPS device, you would not walk in the wrong direction either. This means either you should have a device that tells you the route, or you should already know where the place is located. In the case of our goal, we do not know the exact source of origin. It is not in existence until we achieve it. Our achievement will bring our goal into existence. Thus, discipline has such potentiality to get a thing from imagination to reality. All activities that formed a discipline are like an infinite dot that forms a circle or a line on paper. Have a goal, make a plan, and set up some personal rules related to your short-term and long-term goals. There will be some time when you get tired of staying inside a boundary created by your laws; during such moments, analyse your activities, efforts, and the outcomes.

If you are still not happy with them, there must be something wrong with your goal. Study your goal, gather information, meet people of similar goals, learn how they are moving forward, and then reconstruct another effective model of your discipline. Since we are born free, it is implausible that your mind will accept all restrictions that you created for yourself. However, once you realize the rules are not meant to harm you but to strengthen you, your mind will start enjoying the restrictions, and thus, a new habit of a successful person is formed.

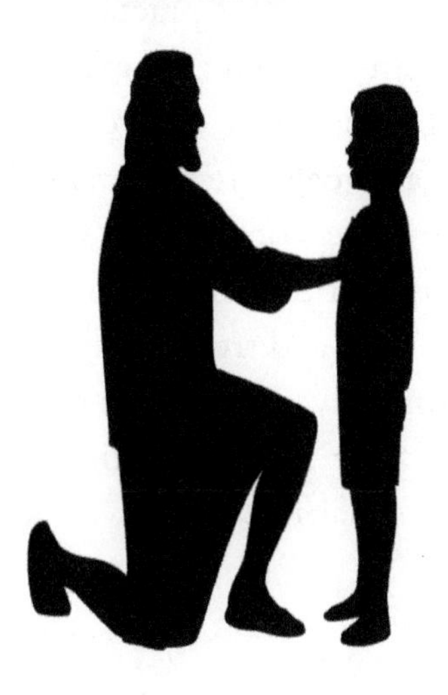

Summary Of Chapter XIII

Discipline can be considered as a bridge that will take you to your goal. That bridge is not established until you have strong willpower. Willpower gets strengthen via patience. If there is no goal, the bridge leads to nowhere; no bridge will be constructed to reach nowhere. I mean, there will be no existence of a bridge without the presence of the goal. After building the bridge, a man should have the willpower to overcome the fair of height to walk on it. Once a person starts walking on the bridge, he should have the patience that he is going to reach his goal in some time; he should not return halfway or give up because of some crisis or issues. Anything we decide to achieve in our life requires us to work hard. We need to know where to put our time and effort. Discipline will provide us the correct direction to reach our goal without getting lost in the middle of the journey. Every dream has specific demands and hindrances to overcome. Becoming a singer and a boxer is a different type of goal. They need their particular discipline. The discipline of one may not be applicable for another. A boxer practicing to sing in a higher octave will not help him to win an upcoming fight. Neither a singer learning kick-boxing will make him win a singing competition. Likewise, all goals are different, but the amount of diligence they require can be comparable. On the other hand, just writing a dream and not even thinking about carrying it out will not help you. Live with your rules and try to make it as flexible as possible but never make it useless. If you are walking towards the East with full enthusiasm, where your goal is, with a GPS device that is discipline, loaded with unshakable willpower and patience, you are invincible.

1. **Wake-up: 6 A.M.**
2. **Drink water, sip by sip.**
3. **Write dream tracking journal.**
4. **Drink the boiled water with my recipe.**
5. **Practice deep breathing in an open area.**
6. **Chant the mantra you created.**
7. **Physical exercise, flexibility, and Chess game**
8. **Practice visualization (does not have to be in the morning).**
9. **Be kind, and practice the willpower in as many activities as possible.**
10. **Eat healthy and detach yourself from unnecessary desires.**
11. **Exercises to find the reason of your existence.**
12. **Change your attitude towards the money.**
13. **Be courageous**
14. **Read a paragraph every day; non-fiction books**
15. **Self-hypnosis before bed/anytime.**
16. **Chant the mantra you created before bed.**
17. **Learn something new every day.**
18. **Stay alone and practice silence for 10min every day.**
19. **Free-writing 3 min a day.**
20. **Discipline; make some rules that connects you with your goal.**

CHAPTER XIV

BREAK THE BOUNDARIES

"Only the truth of who you are, if realized, will set you free."-
Eckhart Tolle

Have you ever seen a pack of wolves reacting to a wolf from a different pack? Acceptance of a stranger or intruder in a pack is not casual. How about bees from other hives? Bees from each hive are coated with a specific chemical that separates them from one another. This is why a bee from one hive cannot enter another hive unless the guard bees allow them. The guards will allow them to enter only if the hives are close to each other. We may think that all ants we see on the ground from the same species can live harmoniously in any colony. No, if the lost ant doesn't share the same pheromone scent as the ants from the new territory, the stranger will be rejected and killed by other ants regardless of their species. All living organisms tend to form a group of their own kind, except some creatures that live in loneliness. A member of a group cannot easily join another group regardless of their species. There are some criteria to be fulfilled if one group member wants to get into another group. For example, let's talk about ants. If intruder ants can spray themselves with the required scent of the colony, they will be accepted in the colony. Thus, all organisms are divided among themselves into different groups, and they can be hostile when those other groups come face to face. It is not practically possible to form a single pack of wolves globally, a single colony of all similar species of ants, or one giant hive of all bees that live worldwide. Are we humans different from those creatures? Is it possible for a human to break the boundary of any group?

If aliens watch us from the sky, they may think we all human as a single unit, but in reality, humans have more divisions within the species than any other organisms. Ants from the same colony, at least, perform as a single unit, but humans living in the same community are divided into various groups in the name of colors, race, social status, religions, social groups or clubs, nationality, and as many divisions as they can form. If a person is not a member of a specific social group or religious firm, he is less like to get help in need. Even if some groups come forward for assistance, the group wants him to be a group member. In other words, we need to apply a particular type of scent to get accepted in the colony created by a group of humans. Whether it is in the deep dark Amazon Forest or in the chaotic city of New York, groupism utterly exists; a person always looks for a group closest to the group he belonged to. A new Chinese guy in New York must likely look for a Chinese community to live in the city. So does an Indian guy, or Hispanic guy, or any other person of a different race. A Christian person prefers the Christian community, and so do other religions followers.

I noticed a pattern of human nature in selecting his team for hangout when I was in the basic training of the US Army. In training, I met an Indian friend, and he told me that he was eyeballing every day to see if there were anybody from the same nationality background in the battalion to have someone share his feelings on training. I saw a few Chinese soldiers making their own small group, and all Hispanic soldiers were in the same group regardless of the country of their originality. African Americans had a separate hangout team, and white soldiers were together in a small group. African soldiers were hanging out with us, Indians, Nepalese, Arabic. When we humans go to a new place, we are more inclined to look for people who share our common background. First, we check our nationality background. If it does not match, we go for the closest quality to match; we look for the person from the neighboring country like the Indian friend was happy to see me because we would share a similar background. If nothing matches, we look for the status; if the person is born a citizen or an immigrant. All immigrants stay together regardless of their race, color, religious belief, and language. By all means, we humans are different in so many ways. But naturally and biologically, we are the same. Humans are the only creature that does not have more than one species. If we look at other animals such as birds, dogs, cows, insects, fishes, etc., they have several species. For example, there are thousands of different species of birds in the world. For the human, there are only one species known as Homo Sapiens at the present time. Despite belonging to the same species, we all humans have divided our unity into smaller parts. As a result, a person belongs to some groups or boundaries before realizing that he is free and only belongs to humanity.

Why do we have so many groups? Ants, bees, or other species living in the same colony or hive do not have various sub-division within the group. Only we with higher consciousness have a tendency to use reasoning to divide the race into several fragmentations. We can create or destroy any division and sub-division of human-created groups. There are more than 4200 estimated religions globally, and they may come under other main religions. This means, within the same religion, there are different groups and their values. Jean-Jacques Rousseau once said, "A man is born free, and everywhere he is in chains." But a man, when he is born, he is not free; he is bound by the fate of the family where he is born. If he is born in a Christian family, he is a Christian by default. When he makes his own decision and jumps out of the religious box, he automatically falls into another box. He replaces the old religious group with a new similar one or entirely different group. Even if he completely deserts all religions of the world, he falls into a group of Atheists. It is nearly impossible to escape these groups.

We are attracted to specific groups based on our belief system. Our belief system is constructed with the way we are brought up. A person can break the belief system and come out of it but cannot wholly free himself from the entire group system of social life unless he knows the secret of how to do it.

Let us suppose that there is an infinite water body just like an ocean. An endless number of aquariums with different sizes are situated on the bottom of it.

For the fishes living in aquarium A, their entire world is not bigger than the size of the aquarium itself. Suppose each aquarium is infinitely large and can contain an infinite number of fishes. In this case, all fishes living in that aquarium share the same resources. If a fish from aquarium B manages to enter aquarium A, fish B will experience an entirely different world. The shapes of both aquariums may be different. So, assuming that fishes are intelligent and would recognize the difference. Let's say that all aquariums are interconnected with tunnels, and fishes can move around to several aquariums. Every time they get into a new aquarium, they experience a new world; some world may be larger than other. If they live in the same aquarium for their entire life, they will end up believing that nothing exists outside those aquariums. If some fishes manage to break the aquarium and come out of it to the vast ocean instead of moving around the aquariums, they will enjoy the vast water, resources, and freedom. Now, let's see this aquarium effect of the human mind.

Humans have created many mental aquariums that compelled us to remail inside of one of these. I have noticed a lot of people changing religions nowadays. From Hindu to Christians, Christians to Muslims, Muslims to Buddhists, and vice-versa. If you have been grown up with a particular religious belief and continued living with that belief for 20 yrs. and all of a sudden, you convert into another religion. Since you were dissatisfied with the previous one, you have a higher chance to love the new belief system. A lot of things you come across there will be new to you. As a result, you will find this new religion more practical, robust, and appealing. If this fact is wrong, why is the conversion of faith is on both ways? I have seen Christians converted into Hindus and Hindus converted into Christians. If one aquarium contains the truth and all other are fake, then why all aquariums are full of people. How people find peace in all belief systems? If one Christian gets converted into Hindu, he feels like he found the secret of the universe. Similarly, the feeling of new converted Christians is the same. This is only an example related to religions. We have created numerous mental aquariums to enclose ourselves, such as feminism, transgenderism, politics, clubs, humanitarian teams, etc.

In my second deployment to the Middle East in 2019, I met a soldier who was not happy to live a normal life; he sought to be spiritually awakened. He was an enthusiastic person of around 19 years of age. Though he was not from my company and my own soldiers, I invited him to join the training class that I had conducted to set a higher goal, money, and investment every Thursday evening. I was looking forward to him. He missed two consecutive classes. The next time when I met him, I asked for the reason for his absence. At first, he was not open to talking about it. When I motivated him to speak openly, he told me that he was getting into a non-religious social group, and its preaching was also on the same day and same time. The other week, he told me that he was taking a bible study class, and he accepted that he was lying. Both weeks, he was in the preaching class of the group. He was a hardcore Christian before, and he was dissatisfied with it. Therefore, he was trying to test the taste of another group that has a different set of beliefs. That day I explained this concept of the aquarium to him. By the way, I came up with this concept suddenly to make him see the better alternative for achieving peace and reaching out for the higher consciousness.

We are highly imaginative creatures, and we create numerous hallucinating worlds inside our minds. Our brain does not see the actual world as it is. It receives the reflected light from the object, and an inverted image is created in our retina, and other parts send the signals in the form of electrochemical signals, which are delivered to the brain, and then we see things. So, the reality is just an electrochemical signal going to the brain. Any impaired parts of our eyes and brain can transform the realities into illusions. Those electrochemical signals can be triggered due to some reasons. As a result, a person may see things that are not in existence. Similarly, we have created our own world in our minds based on the information we were fed. We see the external world as our inner world is. If we are depressed inside, the outside world means nothing to us; we won't be able to see beyond the boundary we created for ourselves, and even if we see it, we interpret it in our own way. The reality does not matter for us; we decide what is not reality. It's like looking at the clouds and seeing different shapes in them. When a person is unhappy despite having all sorts of comforts or without having any of them, he seeks an outlet to reach somewhere where he can find those things he always wishes for. In the quest to appease his mental thirst, he jumps from one aquarium to another. All aquariums are mental boundaries, and they have their own set of beliefs and rules. Some aquariums may offer a wide range of freedom, and some may demand a strict following of its path. When a person jumps from one aquarium to another, he may find the pleasures for some time, but it will not last long because the boundary is a boundary. No limitation is comparable with the ultimate freedom, no matter how large it is. He may move around from square aquarium to triangular one or from rectangular to cylindrical, but the issue follows him everywhere. If a person is unsatisfied with his mental boundary, he should break the border and never get into another. Many atheists believe that they do not belong to any group or aquariums. When they think that there is no God, they already fall into an aquarium of a disbeliever. Those aquariums not only represent beliefs and faith, but they also represent a fragmentation of humans in race, color, status, nationality, and so on. In the picture above, the size of the aquariums is different, but also the entities that live in them are various as well, mentally. A person from 'A' may not be welcome in 'B' and vice versa easily. Like all ants living in the same colony have specific scents, all humans of similar belief systems like each other.

As you start the spiritual journey, you have a chance of having one of the three mentalities:

1. The value of the teaching of all aquariums is the same.
2. All could be fine, but mine is the best.
3. All are different, and to know the truth, we should learn something from all.

The first mentality of seeing all religions the same or all humans regardless of race, color, or nationality is definitely a sign of spiritual awakening. However, there is a slight problem with this mentality, and that is it still maintains a boundary. It tries to include all smaller aquariums, but the box remains a box even after adding all areas. A person who is a saint by nature falls in this category. They view the world as a giant aquarium and all humans as their brother and sister. They personally do not jump from aquarium to aquarium but assume that all aquariums offer the same resources and peace of mind. In their aquariums, a person from 'A' is no different from another person from 'H.' It is like all ants in the world living in the same huge colony.

The second mentality arises when a person is highly educated about his aquarium. In this situation, he condemns the existence of other aquariums. He believes that there is only one actual aquarium. He has never visited another aquarium but assumes that his world is the best. The existence of some other aquariums does not matter to him. If he encounters someone from a different aquarium, he will never understand the point of view of the new person. It is terrible to have this kind of arrogant attitude, but on the positive side, at least he does not have thousands of other aquariums to break if he wants to be free. But the faith of this type of person toward his aquarium is so strong that it is almost impossible to make him know that the world is more extensive than his aquarium.

The third mentality tells us about optimism. This type of person believes in everything and tries to find the truth from every possible solution. We see people from this aquarium so often in our daily life. They are gullible. They enclose themselves into so many mental aquariums that breaking all of them becomes almost impossible. In the religious world, these people are known as seculars. The difference between the 1st concept and the 3rd is people who belong to the 3rd concept tend to follow what all religions say and celebrate all festivals with equal enthusiasm. These people connect themselves to several groups and associations. They think at least one is the ultimate truth, and they will eventually get a pass from heaven.

Have you ever thought about not falling into any of those categories? The secret behind the enlightenment is to know what to look for after breaking the aquarium.

"Are you enlightened?" He asked me.
That was a vague question. I was quiet.

As humans, we need to break all boundaries and mental aquariums instead of jumping from one box to another. They are jails from the point of view of the truth. We should not force ourselves to get captured in such prisons. After breaking the aquarium, you are enclosed with, you will see the world in its proper form, and there will be no brainwashing and no hallucination. Breaking the boundary may be easy but cleansing the mind requires a method. Just saying you do not belong to any aquarium does not mean anything; you need to prove that you have successfully smashed the aquariums.

Summary Of Chapter XIV

When we have issues, we need to reach the root and find the solution. But we often get impatient, and instead of finding a proper solution for inner turmoil, we tend to satisfy our minds externally; we join different clubs and religious teams in the hope of finding the appropriate answer to our problems. Instead, we get ourselves moved from one mental aquarium to another. True happiness is there when we are free. Our mind is always enclosed in some boundaries; we need to free it. When we release our minds, we will see the world as it is. We need no filter to see the truth of the world. However, our mind has several filters through which reality alters. Those filters are made up of faith and beliefs; we need to destroy them. The quest of finding the truth starts only after you successfully break your boundary. Remaining inside an aquarium, you will only experience the altered version of reality. No matter how much you are knowledgeable, you will never see what is not in your aquarium. Trust me, breaking the human-created boundaries won't make you faithless. Instead, it will show you what to trust and give you the path that leads you to the cosmic consciousness. Wake up, open your eyes, and feel the mental aquariums around you; BREAK THEM!!!

1. **Wake-up: 6 A.M.**
2. **Drink water, sip by sip.**
3. **Write dream tracking journal.**
4. **Drink the boiled water with my recipe.**
5. **Practice deep breathing in an open area.**
6. **Chant the mantra you created.**
7. **Physical exercise, flexibility, and Chess game**
8. **Practice visualization (does not have to be in the morning).**
9. **Be kind, and practice the willpower in as many activities as possible.**
10. **Eat healthy and detach yourself from unnecessary desires.**
11. **Exercises to find the reason of your existence.**
12. **Change your attitude towards the money.**
13. **Be courageous**
14. **Read a paragraph every day; non-fiction books**
15. **Self-hypnosis before bed/anytime.**
16. **Chant the mantra you created before bed.**
17. **Learn something new every day.**
18. **Stay alone and practice silence for 10min every day.**
19. **Free-writing 3 min a day.**
20. **Discipline; make some rules that connects you with your goal.**
21. **Break the aquariums.**

CHAPTER XV

ARE YOU READY?

"When the student is ready, the teacher will appear. When the student is truly ready, the teacher will disappear."
- Tao Te Ching

You asked, now, you will be given. You knocked at the door; the door will be opened. You desired to be changed. Now, the change will undoubtedly happen. You decided to shed the personality you had, and you just did it. Now, a new enthusiastic personality will empower your soul. Power comes with responsibility so does the change. Changes not only bring opportunities but also challenges. Now, you have the eyes to see opportunity through the obstacles. Your energy level is changed, and now, you are vibrating at the upper level. You have the keys to your subconsciousness, and you are the creator of your own reality. When you have eyes that are comfortable to see in the light, you are not bound to live in the darkness anymore, and if you have broken all mental aquariums effectively, you may find yourself alone in the further journey. Slowly, you will move on, and things around you will be left behind; the people you used to hang around may find it uncomfortable to be around you. Your new vibration will decide which frequency to attract. Everything vibrating in harmony with your old being will be left behind because now, you are in the journey of greatness. There is a chance that you will be ridiculed, left alone, embarrassed, and condemned every step of your trip; they are nothing but chisels and hammers that are trying to turn you into a beautiful statue. Shrug off the pain; do not complain. Is your willpower strong enough to get you back on your feet after being knocked down several times by the punches of adversity? You chose the more challenging path, but success is inevitable. You may lose your old identity, comforts, and relationships. It may be a shame if you bounce back to the same old level with failures. Do you have the patience to withstand the starvation of your progress? Are you ready?

After practicing all these exercises repeatedly, an alteration in the person's behavior is inexorable. A person will vibrate with a higher energy level and behave so that a brand-new personality is formed. The reality for him is not distorted anymore because he will use his inner eye to see the world. An infinite change will occur in a person during this spiritual metamorphosis process. However, the experiences will be varied from person to person. Some of the significant changes in a person after following the instructions of this book are discussed below. These are the observation I and some of my students personally experienced as the outcome of the regular practice.

Emotional Change

At the beginning of the spiritual metamorphosis process, you may most likely outburst with any form of emotion. You may cry or laugh or be pleased for no reason. The type of emotional outburst may refer to the internal building block of your emotional world; if you have gathered too much pain in the past, you may incline to cry. But crying may occur due to several reasons; you really do not to suffer to shed tears. The feeling of ecstasy can make you cry with joy too. Since you know the fact of "Drasta bhava", nothing can manipulate your emotions. However, sometimes we may be fooled by the situation and get compelled to react so that later on, we feel less awaken for getting manipulated so easily. I remember an incident of such category that I experienced in the summer of 2014. I was working in the physics lab of Idaho State University part-time. Thus, I had plenty of time for myself. I started meditating in the graveyard, a few miles away from my apartment. I chose the cemetery because there was a lot of vegetation and wildlife. Besides, there would be no disturbances in the grave because living people usually do not visit the grave, and the dead cannot make noises to distract me. My meditation start time would be at 0700 every day, and I would set up an alarm for 1000. The alarm was necessary because sometimes I get so deep into meditation that I would lose the sense of time. It was Sunday morning. I was facing the opposite direction of the grave and sitting on Siddhasana pose nearby a bush, a little further away from woods. A few minutes after I closed my eyes, I heard the disturbing chirping of birds in the bush. I tried to concentrate, but there was no avail of trying. I finally opened my eyes to see what was wrong with them. They never disturbed me before when I was meditating a few meters away from that specific location. They might have perceived me as a threat to them. I looked at my phone. It was 0925; two and half hours were passed, but I felt like I closed my eyes for 10 min only. I turned around and saw 5 to 7 birds sitting on the branches of bush and yelling (chirping) as loud as possible. As soon as I turned around, they started behaving weirdly; they flew back and forth in random directions. I ignored their behavior and closed my eyes again. They started flying above me, and their shouting got even louder. Then, there was no point in closing my eyes and force myself to meditate.

All of a sudden, I remembered an incident that happened to my sister a long time ago. My sister was brushing her teeth on the terrace of her house. She heard the chirping of a bird. That bird kept approaching her, and when my sister looked at it, it was flying slowly toward the wall of the terrace. My sister ignored the bird a few times. But when the bird persisted, she was compelled to follow the bird a few steps. When she was guided to the wall, she saw that a crow was invading the bird's nest and was trying to eat the eggs. My sister threw rocks at the crow and saved the bird's family. My mind instantly suggested that I follow the instinct and tell me to listen to the birds. I looked at the birds; we had eye contact. They flew to the nearer tree. I followed them as soon as I reached the tree, they flew towards another one. By that time, I had already realized that they were leading me somewhere. After following them for 300 to 400 meters in the wood, they started chirping loud. I saw many birds of similar species flying around a tall tree. One bird that led me there flew straight to a branch that was at 20 more feet. I saw a big owl holding a bird on its claw. The bird was not dead and was still struggling to survive. I assumed that the bird which tried to hit the Owl in my presence must be the mate of the captured one. As soon as I saw that, my human nature of helping awoke, and I picked up a few rocks. I missed the target twice. In the third trial, I succeeded in hitting the Owl; I heard the collision sound. It was not hard enough to bring the Owl down because I did not want to hurt Owl. Owl turned its head 180 degree and stared at me. I was mad and emotionally driven. I stared at its eyes. Instantly, I felt like I understood what Owl was telling me. "It is my food for my babies and me." Now, I was crushing between two feelings; whether to help birds or let Owl feeds its babies or satisfies its hunger. I chose to help birds. I threw another rock and hit the target successfully. The Owl flew to the next branch and turned its body towards me. It stared at me with wide scary eyes. As I was reaching for another rock, various thoughts crossed my mind.

A strong is always dominating the weak ones. Owl was stronger than those smaller birds, so it was killing them and me, humans stronger than Owl. Thus, I was trying to interfere with their business. What is the difference between an Owl and me? I put myself in Owl's position and realized that the bird, which is a bird to me, is just food to the Owl. The point of view was different. Then, I should leave the Owl alone. But what about the birds who came for my help? If they know a human can get them out of trouble, and what would they think of me when I turned them down? They definitely have feelings and a sense of making a proper decision; I watched personally. I put myself in the place of the birds. How would I feel if someone kills my family member and the messiah, I brought to help us leaves us to die? Mixed feelings overwhelmed me, and an uncontrollable stream of tears fell out of my eyes. I could not stop myself from crying. I stood there for 3-5 minutes without being able to decide who to help. Other birds were still flying here and there. They got tired slowly, and without my help, they lost their motivation and hope. I felt so bad for them. I could not stay there any longer. I marched toward my apartment. The thought of gloominess for not being able to help birds hunted me throughout the day. In the evening, I recalled the memory from the morning trying to see what I could do in such a situation. I suddenly remember the state of mind which is called "Drasta bhava". I failed to apply it in the morning. In such a case, any action I take would be wrong. Thankfully, my trials to rescue the bird were unsuccessful. However, I had failed the test. A person who has been meditating for almost a decade should have a good balance of emotions. If the universe was testing my level of awareness, I had failed the test in the morning. When I realized this fact in the evening, I controlled my emotions again, and I discerned the truth of "Drasta bhava" from my own experience. After that, I got determined to apply "Drasta bhava" to those situations where I will be wrong if I take any actions. I learned to act neutral to my emotions.

Thus, when you practice all the mentioned exercises, you open your higher consciousness and become more eligible for positive outcomes, especially for spiritual journeys. You will encounter various changes in your behavior, including the secretion of hormones. You may release more dopamine, the happy hormone, or excessive serotonin, stress hormones, and you will act accordingly. You have to be ready for that. You also need to know how to react to those changes. This is why I included my experience in the above paragraph. If you are driven crazy by your past emotions, shrug it off, cry or do something and get over it. Do not hold it for long; let it go. There are more chances for you to experience appeasing and auspicious thoughts and feelings because you have practiced all the proven exercises from this book. However, if you suffered too much in the past and you were too negative, then you may encounter some unwanted emotions for sure. As your mind changes, the change in sentiment is predestined.

Friend Circle

You will be unfit in your friend circle. If you do not notice it, your friends might. They will feel uncomfortable being around you unless they have spiritually grown up with you in this training period. Assume that you are in a room where there are few of your friends sleeping. But you are awake, freshly awake. Since you are not sleeping, but get bored if you do not do anything to entertain yourself. You start walking around in the room. You sing and dance and stay happy. But the problem is you are the only one who is awake in the room. A person who is awake for long will definitely disturb the sleepers. Your friends will kick you out of the room; they will feel uncomfortable and annoyed when you are in the room. Similarly, if you are spiritually awake, you will bother others who are not awake. Thus, the chance of them getting away from you is high. You may experience difficulty in getting along with your family members. I am not saying that you will have unnecessary arguments. However, your mental vibration will repel others who are not vibrating at your level. Do not feel alone if this happens to you because it is a positive sign of your progress physically and mentally. Therefore, are you ready to be lonely from now?

Changes In Thinking Pattern

Even if there is no profound change in your physical body, your inner world will temporarily change. The thinking pattern you had earlier would either be polished or layered by a unique way of thinking. You will start seeing the world in your own way. You may understand things with less effort, and you can view items from a different perspective. When something happens, you will not only be able to see the real cause but also will be able to solve it via first principles. Your new thinking skill may put you in arguments so often because others may not be able to perceive the things you can see. From the perspective and the mechanism and functions of things, you may have a different opinion than others. Your way of thinking can bring a different perspective to any issues you see. Now, your thoughts won't be superficial. Your profound contemplative nature will try to solve the problems from the root. You will start creating new realities as your thinking pattern is changing. The more you read, the better your thinking pattern will be. When you see a problem, you may be able to see the consequences of it two or three steps ahead; your brain will automatically connect dots. I mean, your brain will try to compare the issue with anything you knew before. If it is entirely new, the brain will use imagination from the images we have stored in the memory to forecast the most probable future. It is just like playing chess. When you play chess for a long, you can easily predict the outcomes of every single move of your opponent and can possibly save your pieces. Similarly, just by seeing the problem, you will, at least, be able to prevent it from becoming more devastating.

Impact On Lifestyle

You will live a different way of life than before. To be able to experience and get as much as you can out of this book is being disciplined. You will have to wake up at a specific time, eat and fast in a particular way, do physical and mental exercises, play chess, and adhere to most of the principles discussed in the book for 45 days. Automatically, your lifestyle will be different within 3 weeks of practice. This is the process of becoming a magnet of health, wealth, and wisdom, and you may start seeing the effect of the knowledge of this book before you finish 45 days of practice. Even if you feel that you are not becoming a magnet within one or two weeks, your life will be changed regardless of what you think about this book. You will start vibrating at a different frequency. If you used to go to the bar and listen to loud music, try again after 45 days, you will hate it and repel that frequency. You will soon run away from any type of unhealthy vibrations. It is not because of your conscious mind; it is because of your subconscious level.

Belief System

Any belief system we create in society is no other than creating an aquarium to enclosed ourselves because we feel safer staying inside the borderline we made. The belief system here refers to the religious boundary and all boundaries we create in our minds. Self-image is also a firm boundary that prevents us from daring something unusual in our life. We all have some sort of belief system that determines our actions and behaviors. If you persistently search for the answers instead of accepting the beliefs and faiths as the answers, you have a high chance to break the bubbles of these illusions. When you sharpen your mental agility by clearing as many misconceptions as possible, focus and concentration power will rise. All we need for the accomplishment of the goal is the focus, determination, and diligence.

Those are some of the apparent changes that occur within you within 45 days. You are becoming more capable, and thus more challenges will come to you. If you can break as many aquariums as you can, you expose yourself to more and more uncertainty, the uncertainty of attracting unpredictable things into your life. As a result, your life tends to be boring from the outside and more thriller from the inside. Following is some of the situations you may have to pass through to be mentally tough.

Feeling Of Restlessness

Though you may not be physically busy, your mind will be restless. You may not find peace on anything. You may feel down but may not know the reason. This is the confusing state of your mind. At this point in time, your mind is trying to fall back into the same frequency level that you used to have before you started the training. But the new habit you just established by the exercise will push you up by motivating you to vibrate in the same higher energy level. Many people failed to motivate themselves or lack consistency in training, resulting in their fall back into the same old energy level.

Feeling Of Detachment:

I do not want you to get detached from everything and become a monk. This is why I included the chapters such as wealth and courage. We really do not need to abandon our family, wealth, or other general social status to achieve greatness in the spiritual world. Of course, less distraction is the best for meditation. But it is easy to have peace in the forest where you may vibrate with the frequency of peace quickly, but the greatness is there if you can vibrate with peace in the presence of people in the city. Silence does not mean peace, and noises do not necessarily mean violence. However, there is a high chance of getting the feeling of detachment. You may want to live a monk life. Your inner consciousness may tell you to renounce everything. If you have family and kids, your responsibility towards them is the first thing you need to worry about. Leaving family and society because of failure in social life is not valid. Live two lives together; spiritual and materialistic. Give 100% of yourself when you are in the character of either one of the lives.

Seeking A Higher Goal

Some unknown sadness within you will continuously hunt you. You will not find the proper reason for it. This may happen because your inner consciousness knows what it wants, but there is confusion at a conscious level. Or your subconscious mind is not happy with what is happening in the present. You will need to read something similar to the goal you set up earlier. You may have to hang out with people with a similar purpose. Every time you encounter such feelings, just go on a short walk; it activates your mind enabling it to think more effectively. Your inner consciousness continuously processes towards your life's purpose, and if you do not act accordingly, it gets upset. You need to give a meaning to your life, at least a higher goal so that your subconscious mind will be busy with positive tasks.

Losing Interests

This is one of the most common feelings that you are going to experience. As you are learning new skills, discouraging thoughts will arise in your mind. On the other hand, you may start viewing everything as useless. When you are in the phase of spiritual awakening, everything outside may mean nothing to you. You will lose interest in mediocre activities which are not related to your goal. You may lose interest in the source of entertainment and social media as well. The chances of losing interest in the materialistic world get higher as you are more involved in spiritualism. However, if you become successful in focusing on worldly life more and balancing both parts of life, you may create a peaceful atmosphere in and out of your mind.

Love Loneliness

When you become your own best friend, you may love to stay away from the crowd. You may find it boring and useless to hang around aimlessly. You will be likely to cut down the friend circle. You will incline to learn more than hanging around and pass the time with friends. You will love peace and less noise. You will start enjoying your own company more than any other source of entertainment. Especially when you make a habit of reading and writing, you will spend more time with yourself. The good thing about being alone for you in this stage is you are not pessimistic anymore, and you will never harm yourself while vibrating with a better energy level. You may feel sad in a positive way but not in a depressive way. Even if you feel sad, you will push yourself to progress in your dream because you know the reason for your sadness and know how to eradicate such feelings.

Summary Of Chapter XV

If there is action, there will be a reaction too. If you practice most of the exercises discussed in this book, the universe will undoubtedly react to your actions. Your present decisions and actions have the intensity to override your past experiences and create new realities favorable to your wellbeing. When your willpower gets more robust, the concentration power gets amplified. With this high level of concentration, anything you desire will have to turn into reality. However, in making wishes into reality, your inner consciousness goes through a debate between the conscious and subconscious minds. As a result, you will see a lot of confusion and changes in your life. The changes and chaos will occur temporarily. You will have to practice more to make the effects permanent. Slowly, your lifestyle will be changed, and you may find your mind way more restless than usual. You may act differently, and your new personality can shock others. You may sound more matured and more imaginative to others. Your temper may take over you, and you may react in violence. The flow of energy within your body will be up and down. You may be enthusiastic at a time and lose interest in doing anything next. Your behavior will change unexpectedly. In the beginning phase, your changed behaviors will bring uncertainty and undesirable results. You should be ready for all impending consequences from today onwards.

1. **Wake-up: 6 A.M.**
2. **Drink water, sip by sip.**
3. **Write dream tracking journal.**
4. **Drink the boiled water with my recipe.**
5. **Practice deep breathing in an open area.**
6. **Chant the mantra you created.**
7. **Physical exercise, flexibility, and Chess game**
8. **Practice visualization (does not have to be in the morning).**
9. **Be kind, and practice the willpower in as many activities as possible.**
10. **Eat healthy and detach yourself from unnecessary desires.**
11. **Exercises to find the reason of your existence.**
12. **Change your attitude towards the money.**
13. **Be courageous**
14. **Read a paragraph every day; non-fiction books**
15. **Self-hypnosis before bed/anytime.**
16. **Chant the mantra you created before bed.**
17. **Learn something new every day.**
18. **Stay alone and practice silence for 10min every day.**
19. **Free-writing 3 min a day.**
20. **Discipline; make some rules that connects you with your goal.**
21. **Break the aquariums.**
22. **Be ready for emotional breakdown and uncertainty.**

CHAPTER XVI

MEDITATION

"Truth is the offspring of silence and meditation."
- Isaac Newton

Meditation has a history of thousands of years in human civilization. However, the western world was incognizant of the practice until the 1700s. Meditation flourished in the world of the west when the Eastern philosophical textbooks were translated into different European languages. Books such as Vedanta, Upanishads, Bhagavad Gita, and Buddhist Sutras played a significant role in disseminating the seed of meditation in western countries. Meditation became more prominent in the United States in 1893 when Swami Vivekananda visited the Parliament of Religion in Chicago. His presentation enchanted thousands of Americans' hearts and opened the door for other spiritual teachers to see the United States. He lived in the US for two years and spread the knowledge of Vedic philosophy. After him, Swami Rama Tirtha visited the US in 1902 and preached about Vedanta for almost two years, and in 1920 Paramahansa Yogananda enlightened American people about the Eastern philosophy of yoga. In the 1960s, Swami Prabhupada founded the International Society for Krishna Consciousness in the US. Gurudev Dr. Narayan Dutta Shrimali, founder of Mantra-Tantra-Yantra Science, my spiritual guide, visited the US in 1986. I heard about the following story of him when I was a kid. The following information is derived from the Mantra-Tantra-Yantra Science blog, siddhashram.blogspot.com.

"In December 1986, Param Pujya Gurudev Dr. Narayan Dutta Shrimali was invited for addressing gatherings in six places in America on "Sun Principle and transformation of matter." This article was written by Mr. Brevian, a famous American journalist and one of the sternest critics of India at that time, covering the final session of Guruji's program in Washington, capital of the United States.

Despite the cold temperature in December in America causing a cold response in public gatherings, either political or art and dance exhibition, the news of an Indian presenting practical program on "Sun Principles" in five prominent USA cities was verbally spreading amongst enthusiasts. It was noted that the said Indian was not after any financial gain nor had a desire for fame. His just intended as a Vedic knower was to demonstrate and introduce the art of the ancient Vedic science called Surya Vigyan or "Sun Principal" for the first time in history to the Western public.

The purpose was apparent that in the modern scientific era of the 20th century, he wanted to prove that it would be possible to convert and transform one matter into another by tapping solar energy. In other words, according to him, without using any form of hypnotism or magic, you can actually convert a simple piece of cotton into a bit of hard rock.

Impossible!! Utterly Impossible!

If it were mere possible, the whole world would dash into a devastating of a chaotic revolution, as people will be converting iron into gold and could, in this way, gain simply anything. If it would be merely possible, it would actually be one of the most phenomenal scientific achievements of the current century. However, in this matter, it was my assigned task to be critical in the utmost matter.

After careful consideration, I formed a committee of eighteen professionals who were selected secretively. Among The eighteen professionals were atomic scientists, Scientists, Physicians, Doctors, Meteorologists, intelligence agents, psychologists, Investigative journalists, solar scientists, Astro-scholar, environmentalists, and Electrical energy specialists. (All names omitted to avoid inaccuracy.)

The professionals I selected were simply the best experts in their fields of work, and I forbid them the following things before the show started:

1. Not to utter any word to the challenger while he is performing
2. Not to show any sign of appreciation.
3. Being utmost critical at all times
4. Not to communicate with each other when the challenger is performing.
5. And finally, of course, be at all times - observing.

The program's venue was set at Jefferson Hall at 3 clocks, for one hour period. The platform had a seating capacity of one thousand the same number of passes/tickets were distributed. But more than 10 thousand people were gathering because Mr. Shrimali's last broadcast was out of six earlier publicized demonstrations.

Mr. Shrimali was sitting on stage and was explaining in fluently English that the sun is the main form of seven different types of rays that can actually create all kinds of matters. All matters are basically made of atoms. If desired, atoms can be created as destroyed or even modified. The modification is actually linked to the transformation of one matter into another. The transformation can be permanent. (Conclusion's quote:)

This knowledge, known as Surya Vigyan (Sanskrit name), can bring revolutionary changes in the medical field. As by example

* Person with weak memory can become more intelligent with the aid of this solar technology applied to certain parts of the brain.

* Unnecessary growth in the body can be destroyed or terminated.
* Kidney stones can be dissolved or discharged with urine,

As indicated, there was total silence in the hall, no clapping nor verbal appreciation, no particular expression on the faces.

Matter Transformation!

I had collected a cubicle piece of wood and a rose flower ready. Washed and cleaned for free of chemical or visible contamination. I have requested Mr. Moore to make sure the challenger does hypnotize the audience. On top of that, we had applied Basil waves in the hall so that hypnotism can be easily deactivated. The program was to be televised live so that people outside the hall could also observe the performance.

We have requested Mr. Shrimali to take off the shirt and garment above the waist, and his dhoti will be checked with special equipment so that nothing will be attached or applied to the dhoti. He will require to wash his thoroughly before the performance, and he was not supposed to move his hands below the waist or touch the dhoti. I have also mentioned to Mr. Shrimali that he will not disclose what material he will be given for matter transformation. He will also not be told what matter he has to transform into. He was only to be notified when he is ready to perform.

At my request, the Environment specialist washed Mr. Shrimali's hands thoroughly and dried them to ensure that the hands are free of any chemical agent(s).

Before that, we have made Mr. Shrimali take off his Kurta (Indian shirt) and Banyan, removed from the stage. Mr. Shrimali stood up in the middle of the stage. Raised his hands above his head that he was all clear and said: you can see my hands, and you can see they are all empty.

(His bare torso was very attractive)

I took the piece of wood and handed it over to him, and requested him to transform it into gold. After that, I went off the stage and took my seat.

Mr. Shrimali raised his hands, holding the piece of wood in the air, and made a steady look to it.

He started to twist the wood, especially with fingers, and we all were focusing on the piece of wood. One minute passed, two minutes passed, and on the fourth or the fifth minute, we saw the white piece of woodturning its color into golden yellow.

I used my binocular focus on the piece of wood and heard him say: here is the piece of gold, as you desired!

Afterward, I had Mr. Brown look at the gold and hold it separately for a while. Then I got up and handed over the fresh rose flower to Mr. Shrimali and asked him to transform it to iron. Now Mr. Shrimali repeats the same action as before he did with the piece of wood and in two to three minutes, the tender rose transformed into solid iron.

Then Mr. Harwin got up to the stage and went to take a look at the iron rose. The scientists also went to the location to investigate the two transformed items. And after five minutes, they declared that he had succeeded in the challenge and changed both the items into the wanted materials.

The whole hall exploded into appreciation and applause. The tensed faces of the eighteen members relaxed, and each of them went and congratulate Mr. Shrimali. Mr. Shrimali then expresses then his thanks for all his presence there. His voice was full of confidence, polite, and soft spookiness. Mr. Grown handed over the city key for

Washington DC to Mr. Shrimali as an honor. Indeed Mr. Shrimali was the first Indian citizen who got hold of the city key of Washington. I thought, "the Sun indeed has risen in the west.""

I had to paste the above story because it is a piece of an article where the journalist had explained every aspect of his observation. Thus, I could not dare to make it an abridged form of the article. This is how Dr. Narayan Dutta Shrimali demonstrated his power of Siddhi in the western world to prove himself and the power of meditation.

Nowadays, almost everyone knows about the importance of meditation. People want to practice it daily for their well-being. However, there are always a few confusions in our minds regarding meditation. Some of the widespread confusion and questions are listed as below:

Do We Need A Meditation Method?

There is no specific acclaimed method that leads to salvation yet. Several teachers preach about their techniques as the best method, and all religious people believe what they are doing is the most refined form of meditation. Since every individual is different from others from a spiritual level. All of us have monkey minds, but the level of the mischievousness of our minds is different. However, controlling the mind is only the beginning of meditation. Nowadays, many people are stuck in controlling the mind, and they believe that they are meditating. Some people realize that controlling the mind is impossible. So, they prefer watching their thoughts and their breath as the practice of meditation. They claim that there is no need for a meditation method. Is this the actual meditation? It is like a person is told to watch for milk if it boils in the kitchen. He watches it until it boils and wet the floor. What does 'watch' mean in the actual situation? It does not mean to just watch; it means to take appropriate action when requires.

Similarly, meditation does not mean simply watching the thoughts and breathe. There has to be a right action to be taken when the perfect time arrives. The action taken during that time is a method. Meditation comes after the state of no thoughts or control over the mind. The process of clearing thought or just flowing with ideas is not meditation. According to this statement, a vast majority of people are trying to mimic the state of meditation. This is why people like us get stuck in clearing the mind taking it as meditation. As a result, we will never access the siddhis and spiritual accomplishments like Dr. Narayan Dutta Shrimali. According to the Patanjali, a Maharishi who documented yoga sutras around 200B.C., meditation falls on the 7th level of Asthanga yoga. It is like you cannot be a doctor without finishing an undergraduate degree. You need to adhere to all rules and pass-through step by step to get into the level of 'meditation.' If you have read and practiced all exercises mentioned in this book, you are already qualified for learning meditation because this book follows the rules of ashtanga yoga. I have tried to elucidate each activity by providing scientific and academic research papers and personal experiences. However, I will discuss Asthanga yoga in brief here.

'Astha'= Eight
'Anga' = Organ/ part/ limbs
'Yoga' = Union with higher consciousness

By definition, Asthanga yoga has 8 vital organs that make its body. They are:

1. Yama: It is the moral and ethical guidelines to balance the health and well-being of an individual promoting spiritual development. Yama has its 5 sub-division:
    a) Ahimsa: Non-violence
    b) Satya: Truthfulness
    c) Brahmacharya: Celibacy
    d) Asteya: Non-stealing
    e) Aparigraha: Non-covetousness. Possessing what is necessary and avoiding gathering unnecessary stuff.

2. Niyama: It refers to the inner observances, the actions or practice under the requirement of morality and ritual. It has 5 sub-divisions too:
    a) Saucha: Purification of mind; cleansing of thought and feelings. It also means the purification of inner body.
    b) Santosha: Satisfaction of what we have and ability to make things better.
    c) Tapas: Intense self-discipline and willpower.
    d) Swadhyaya: Reading, self-study.
    e) Ishwarapranidhana: Surrender to divine consciousness.

Varuha Upanishads talks about altogether 10 niyamas. So, the remaining of it are:

f) Ksama: Forgiveness
g) Dhriti: Fortitude; courage in pain or struggle or adversity
h) Daya: Compassion
i) Arjava: non-hypocrisy, sincerity
j) Mitahara: Balanced diet

3. Asana: Position.
4. Pranayama: Breathing practice to control over the prana.
5. Pratyahara: Withdrawal of the senses from their objects.
6. Dharana: Concentration, one-pointedness.
7. Dhyana: Meditation.
8. Samadhi: union with divine is achieved.

In the list, you see one exercise comes after another. This means one needs to practice all 6 paths before he reaches the meditation level. But the problem with people nowadays is they want everything fast. They want to buy certificates of training without involving in it. They want to be known as surgeons without going to high school and undergraduate school. Today, to practice as a surgeon, you must have a license. When you practice all six exercises, you will be eligible for meditation. Now, the confusion is what to do at this point in time.

There is no point in observing your breathing at this level because you have already accomplished that level. What to do after it depends upon the goal of meditation. The meditation that is involved with the mantra sadhana will require a specific method to follow. We need a meditation method to achieve a higher state of mind, and there is no doubt. However, there are still a lot of people who do not want to agree on this. They think meditation is natural, and no method is needed. Some powerful techniques such as Tratakas (Gazing exercise) are essential to learn hypnosis and attain more patience and mental power.

If meditation was natural, easy, and methodless, nobody would require an experienced teacher to show the right way, and everybody would be demonstrating 'Astha Siddhi,' which means 8 supernatural powers, in every street. When they have many followers, some spiritual teachers think they can twist the truth and start their own philosophy based on the college degree as their credibility, which is irrelevant to the spiritual world. But they forget that some people have spent their lives experimenting, experiencing, and protecting the ancient meditation methods for the coming generation. They may be hiding in the cave of the Himalayas, or they may be living in a society with zero followers. Whatever the case is, only some lucky persons get to know them and their knowledge; yes, we need a meditation method.

Do We Need A Guru?

A guru is an experienced person who has already done all procedures and reached the climax of the method. They know the positive and negative parts of the path and process. They can also provide the shortcut of the route. When we follow their way, we will not waste our time struggling with unsure methods. When a person manages to reach the 7th level of yoga, he has purified himself and modified himself into a yogi. All individuals are different, but people tend to act the same from their mental level with a shared interest. Thus, a guru can modify a student however he wants. He can devise a new method for students based upon the students' Aura, knowledge, and capacity. Also, he can provide his own path of liberation. One Guru may not possess all knowledge. A student may have to learn a different aspect of yoga from another teacher. A living teacher is better than an ideal textbook. If there is no teacher available, books can be considered a teacher, but the book's teaching is limited. You cannot interact with books.

If you randomly chose the sources such as YouTube and videos from social media to learn meditation, you are likely to achieve nothing. Teachers are the individuals who have already experienced the outcomes and consequences of the method. They have learned from their teachers. Actually, the technique your teacher gives you is a practice that is already scrutinized, experienced, and continued for a long time. The method's accuracy depends upon the teacher's quality, where he learned from, and who his Guru was. Some people announce themselves as Guru. I am not sure about their method. But the ways which can be found in the old text of Eastern Philosophy are trustworthy, and the Guru who has the knowledge about the root sources of meditation are real Gurus. Many people take part in training and feel like they can teach other people about meditation. If somebody has not completed at least 15000 hours of meditation in his life, I would not learn from him; I can listen to him and motivate myself but will never consider him as my teacher. There are still some more characteristics of a capable teacher.

How Would I Know My Method Of Meditation Is Working?

If you meditate regularly, you are more likely to have a curiosity about whether your meditation is working or not. How can you tell if it is working? You may be getting some placebo effects of it, never know. Various people are explaining how it feels when meditation is deep on the internet. Have they really meditated for long enough to claim that, or they just copy-pasted somebody else's experiences? Anyway, you get some motivation out of it; that is what we need. Of course, everyone will have different experiences before, during, and after a deep meditation. However, the emotions related to it will be identical among practitioners at a fundamental level.

BEFORE MEDITATION:

There are two states of mind before meditation:

- **EASE:**
  In this state, our body and mind are calm. We have minimum thoughts, and most of them are positive. We are optimistic and energetic. Usually, this is the time right after you wake up in the morning. However, 90 minutes before sunrise is the most auspicious time to boost up our energy. If you meditate during this hour, you have a higher chance to achieve AFTER MEDITATION effects for the long term in your life.

- **DIS-EASE:**
  In this state of mind, we are overwhelmed with our thoughts. Anger, greed, sex, and all dark thoughts are controlling our behavior. As a result, we get disappointed, and there is a lack of energy and excitement for the next level of our life. We have physical and mental pain. We are ill and have difficulty concentrating on anything. In this condition, all meditation beginners try to meditate to get rid of all of those undesired signs and symptoms, but can anyone eat while running? Usually, this time we are either overjoying or lamenting about how the day went. Also, there is less amount of oxygen at night. So, meditating during this time with a dis-ease feeling could be hazardous, especially meditating without a proper guideline from someone who knows it well.

DURING MEDITATION:

Since we all are mentally different, we will have different physical experiences. However, there are many shared experiences while you are sitting on a posture for the meditation, such as:

MAJOR:

1. Pressure on crown chakras and feeling of heaviness
2. Feeling the flow of the liquid into the spine.
3. Ant like bugs crawling into the spine or in the crown.
4. Immense of light sparkling in the third eye.
5. Numbing of hands, legs, or back.
6. Feeling of coolness or warmness on various part of the body
7. Listening bells or voices
8. Feeling like floating on air and shortened of the breath
9. Experiencing the release of Hormones in the brain, hearing the stream of blood flow
10. Tingling on toes or fingertips as if the current is flowing out, and so on.

MINOR:

1. Heaviness on eyelids
2. Vibrations on the forehead
3. Changes in the heartbeat, and thus, slight changes in body temperature
4. Increment in smelling ability
5. Blockage of one of the nostrils, and so on.

Most of the people who meditate, sitting on a posture, have above experience. When people have those above 'MAJOR' experiences, they think they are succeeding, Aren't they?

Many beginners, even more, experienced ones, take Major experiences (listed above) as their achievement and try to repeat the same process to get the same outcome. Will you reach your destination by running on a treadmill?

When you sit on a posture, crossing your legs, and doing some breathing exercises, all functions of your body will be changed. The center of gravity will change; the free flow of blood, from head to toe, will be disturbed to a certain extent and causes numbness, tingling, change in body temperature, slowing heartbeat, and complete chaos in the system. During that state, our inner system tries to maintain harmony. It will take a few minutes or hours to re-adjust all built-in internal systems while you are sitting.

Then, what about the seeing of bright light and hearing bells or sounds?

Superficially, we think we see with our eyes and hear with our ears, but in reality, our eyes collect light and send it to the brain's visual cortex, where we see the objects or light. The brain already has a pattern of all visuals in the neurons saved in the form of memory. In some cases, it happens to trigger those neurons to activate those electrochemical impulses by which we perceive precisely the same object or light we have seen before. Similar phenomena occur in the case of sound.

Thus, scientifically, it is foolish to accept the above-listed experiences as the success of your practice. You can have those feeling even without practicing meditation and yoga.

AFTER MEDITATION:

If you really want to know whether your practice is in the right direction and whether you are not running onto a treadmill in the name of the spiritual journey, you must have the following symptoms:

1. **Timelapse**

   When you open your eyes, you see the time you spent way more than you planned to sit. The realization of time will have vanished. In the spiritual world, within you, there is no existence of time. Time is human-created, and it is the biggest illusion.

2. **Unconditional Love:**
   As soon as you open your eyes, your heart will fill with ecstasy. You will have unconditional love for everything you see: you may cry, not because of pain, but because of the realization that everything around you is the same. You want to hug them. The trees, rock, ants, bugs, air, cloud, sky, everything you see, you just want to hug them and love them. When the sex disappears from love, there would be no differences among the attachments of how you see your father and your husband. There will be no anger, greed, and desires at this moment.

Summary Of The Chapter XVI

Meditation is a means to appease the psychological pain and a practice that can lead us to supreme knowledge. It enhances memory and also can replace unhealthy cells with healthier ones. A capable teacher appears when the student is ready. But people do not want to work hard, and they only desire the shortcut on everything, which is not possible. Many people avoid accepting the fact that there should be a meditation method. They think just concentrating on things happening around is the meditation, but in reality, that is no close to the experiences of meditation. Many people mimic the state of meditation by sitting in a position and closing their eyes. But meditation requires more than that. The importance of Guru in the spiritual journey is essential. A book can be a teacher but will never be able to replace a real interacting teacher. A student can learn faster with a teacher by avoiding all probable mistakes. Teachers can see if the students are capable of a specific method and the teachers are the one who decides if the students are ready for the upper level. However, today people think that they do not require any teachers to learn meditation. Of course, if you want to see what is happening around you, you really do not need a teacher to see them. But seeing and observing are different from experience. Only an experienced teacher will be able to guide you to the peak of spirituality.

NO EXERCISES FROM THIS CHAPTER:

I promised to make you eligible for the materialistic world and the spiritual journey; I completed my job. From here onward, you have a choice to stop at the material world or keep on moving into spirituality. The material world is an external reality in front of you, and spirituality is the probability you may reach. If you decide to go for possibility, keep on reading related books, and one day you will find your teacher. But until then, you need to practice the exercises I mentioned in this book to purify yourself and prepare for your spiritual journey.

I

DAILY SCHEDULE

This is just an example how a schedule should look like for 45 days. You can modify it as per your need and will. I am not too much concerned about the timetable but about the discipline. Once you design your daily routine, be fixed to it. A flexible schedule is not auspicious for your process of becoming a magnet of health, wealth, and wisdom. All exercises have to be done at the same time every day. For example, you did 'breathing practice' at 0630 on 1st three consecutive days but missed it on the 4th day, or you decided to do it in the evening. You violated the discipline. Don't confuse your conscious and sub-conscious mind unexpectedly. If you missed it after some days of your practice, start until you hit 21 days. After 21 days, even if you miss a day, you do not require to start all over again from day 1. However, If I were you, I would restart from day zero.

The following timetable is just an example for an average household person. If you do not have to make breakfast, lunch, or dinner, you will have a lot of free time. Also, those who do not have a proper job will have an excess amount of time. Thus, you can modify the timetable given in the example according to your availability. When you have plenty of free time, make sure you add extra effort to physical exercises, playing chess, breathing exercises, and reading.

Time	Activities	Duration
600	Wakeup call	
	Drink water sip by sip and write the dream Journal	20min
	Be fresh and get ready for exercises	
630	Physical exercise/ yoga/ flexibility/ running/ walk	20 min
	Breathing exercise	10 min
	Chanting your self-created wish mantra	10 min
	Visualization practice for the fulfillment of your goals	10 min
730	Shower	10 min
	Breakfast and its preparation	20 min
	Getting ready for Job	15 min
900-1730	Work	8-hour 30 min
	Be kind, practice willpower,	
Lunch-break	Play Chess	10 min
	Eat healthy food, contemplate over your plus point to give a purpose to your life	
	Be courageous and truthful	
	Read non-fiction books and learn something new from co-workers every day	
1830	Dinner preparation and eating	40 min
1915	Free- writing practice	3 min
1925	Practice isolation	10 min

1930-2130	Family time	2 hours
2130	Reading	30 min
2200	Bed time, write daily Journal	
	Chant your self-created wish mantra	
	Practice Self-hypnosis for the fulfillment of your desires	Fall asleep

11

CHECKING THE EFFECTIVENESS OF THE PRACTICES DISCUSSED IN THE BOOK

It is very natural for us to doubt the effectiveness of the methods we followed to bring life changes. The confusion is intense when the outcomes are too abstract and cannot be measured physically. Most of the time, people fail to see or measure the consequences of their actions, and they think their efforts were to no avail. If there is action, there must be an equal reaction. But all responses may not fit in our will. If you decide to build a castle in the air, no matter how hard you work to make a wall, it does not stand. Similarly, dumping a hundred gallons of water in the desert hoping to make a pond is not intelligent. In those types of actions, the reaction will be explained by logic but not by the physical consequences. Likewise, if you want to see if this book has worked for you, first of all, you must have completed 45 days of training as discussed in the book. Then, know which part you focused on more. This book talks about aspects of life, such as health, wealth, wisdom, courage, kindness, mind, patience, willpower, etc. All essential exercises discussed in the book are backed up by academic research papers and personal experiences. Besides, thousands of other people follow 'Asthanga yoga' by heart, who have similar experiences.

If you have followed my instruction of writing a daily journal, you can read from the day first to today, you will find the most significant difference in your point of view. Similarly, your physical health should be better already. The feelings of love, affection, peace, kindness, and ecstasy are the first outcomes you may realize. To access the subconscious mindfully for long and creating your own realities may take longer, but it is impending. You may encounter a lot of business ideas or just creative thoughts from out of the blue. This means you have chances to connect with Akashic records where all sorts of knowledge regarding languages, wealth, science, spirituality, and everything about the universe is stored. It is believed that Nikola Tesla, Einstein, Faraday, Thomas Elva Eddison, and so many other scientists receive the idea about their inventions and theories from these universal sources of knowledge. I have personally experienced this fact. I wrote 16 books (just manuscripts; not published) before I turned 14. Each book was completed within one day. I still have a few novels that I did not finish writing in one day; they are still unfinished with 103 pages. This book is on your hand; I am on the 26th day of writing, and I have finished 76,077; two more days to go, and I will be done. For this book, the research part took my time. Otherwise, I would be done writing within 20 days. What I am trying to say is when I write something in any language I know, it pours down to my mind in the form of visuals and experiences. I just have to find a proper word to explain them. If I am writing in the language that I am good at, writing is easy for me. As English is my third/fourth language, I struggle to find the correct word, which slows down my mental observation.

I remember an incident regarding the Akashic record. I had a friend who was one or two years older than me. He was learning composing poems in 'Chhanda.' Chhanda refers to the study of Vedic meter, and people have been using the measurement to set a rule in poetic style. There is an infinite number of Chhanda in Sanskrit poetry. Chhanda not only has a complicated set of rules but also requires a specific style of singing. Each melody is assigned to each Chhanda. This means there is an infinite number of tunes. I had learned Chhanda when I was in high school. One day, four friends were sitting in a tea shop, and he said he took literally 26 hours to write two lines of the poem in 'Anustup Chhanda.' I was surprised because this Chhanda is more straightforward than others, and I suggested that he see the feeling but not force the word without feelings. He did not know I could write in Chhanda too. He had different opinions. To show him what I mean, I composed a poem of 18 lines in 'Upendra Bajra Chhanda,' which is rare, within one hour. But the issue with my poem was the singing part; I was not good at that. It is just about connecting ourselves to the source of cosmic knowledge. When something is exciting to you, you are more likely to get connected with the Akashic records and receive information in the form of blur visuals or feelings. Sometimes, you just keep on writing without the full notice of your conscious mind. Thus, after practicing the exercises from this book, you will access the upper level of mind, eventually giving you the permit of Akashic record. It does not happen quickly, though. You just have to strive for it as you do for one breath while you are drowning.

Watch other people how they are behaving with you; it must be better than before. Are you able to influence more people now? Or you are still a side character in the group of your friend. You should have a ton of courage, and the confidence level must be high. The knowledge you have got from this book and other self-help books should be able to set you apart from the crowd, and you should sound, at least, more intelligent. You may lose old friends and make new friends with a higher vibration and similar goals. Your anger issue must be mitigated by now. Your cells, tissues, organs, system, and entire body should feel rejuvenation, and you should be transforming into a new person already.

If you are still sad, poor, and pessimistic, you know which chapter to revisit. I assure you again that this book can change your life. If I can do it, everyone can do it. I am still following these principles. I get upset sometimes when things do not happen as I desire, but those feelings do not last long. I have strong willpower, which allows me to save or delete memories if I want. Deleting memories is easier for me. If somebody hurts me and I decide not to see them in life, I can permanently erase their memory. I have done this 3 times in my life, and it has worked perfectly. Every time I see them after deleting them from my memory, no feelings occur; they do not exist anymore. This kind of willpower will save you from depression, take your own life, or commit some hideous crimes.

Thus, read the journal you wrote, observe your daily life and realize which part of your life is slacking. When you find the weakest link of your chain, go back to the related chapter, read it over and again. Flood your subconscious mind with similar information, read and write more until you achieve your desire outcomes. Nothing is impossible; even within impossible, there is 'I M POSSIBLE.' It's easy; be positive.

You can predict what will happen in the future based on what is happening right now. Look at the following chart in next page:

Suppose your goal is to be a millionaire, and you are doing some productive activities related to your goal, as shown below in the example. Then, the outcome will likely favor you, and the chances of achieving a goal are higher.

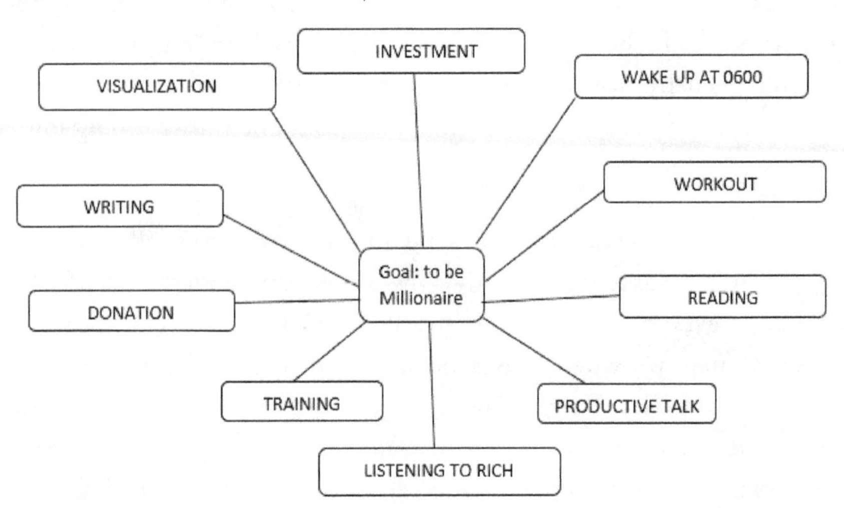

If you are performing the above activities for your goal, the following chart is the probable outcome.

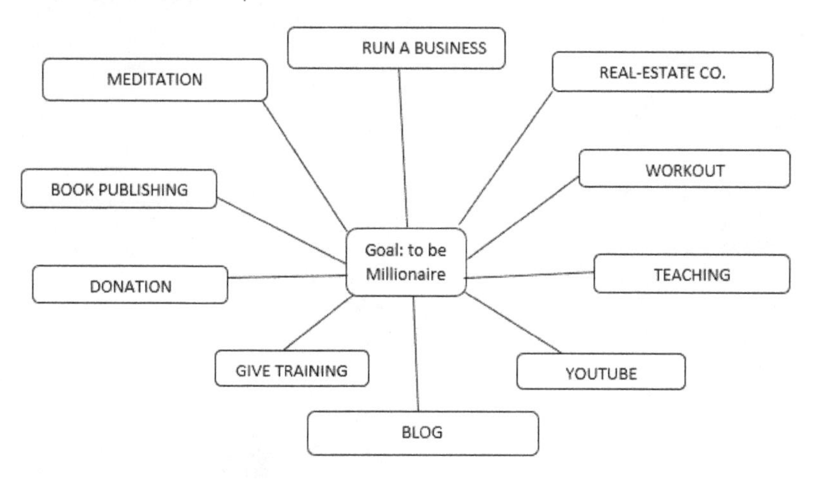

This is just an example of a person with the mindset of becoming a millionaire. If he performs the above-listed jobs in his present times, the second chart is likely to occur. You can have any goal in the center of the chart, but the activities you are doing right now should complement the plan written there. The more you learn and train, the more you get closer to the goal. If you make a chart like this to track your success, it is elementary to locate the mistakes you make in your daily life that keep you away from prosperity. At any confusion or during the lack of motivation, go back to the chapter in this book that gives you motivation or helps you eliminate the delusion. Do not repeat the same activities in the same way after failing at the first attempt. Contemplate over your mistakes, redevise the method of exercise, and move forward. Learn from your presence; how you are feeling right now is the result of yesterday. If you are feeling fantastic today, keep doing what you did yesterday. Have a long-term goal, be positive, diligent, and persistent. Success is knocking at your door. The future healthy, wealthy and wise version of you will thank you for the choice you made today.

III

LAST WORDS

It is the fact that to receive anything in life, we need to be worthy of it. Otherwise, things may come to us and leave with no time. Also, when we receive something that we do not deserve, we either dislike it or lose interest in it very quickly. If the frequency of things does not match yours, the vibration in which your every cell is vibrating will react uncomfortably, and then your mind produces an opposing frequency. As a result, either you get away from the attracted things, or things will slip away from the grasp of your midst. People often talk about getting out of one's comfort zone to face the greater challenges that promote our progress and growth. But getting out of the comfort zone is not as easy as it sounds; it's like diving into the ocean without learning to swim. There may be five out of a hundred who would survive drowning, but 95% would die because of lack of preparation. Getting out of the comfort zone means trying to reach a higher energy level or different state of mind, and if one does not know how to achieve such level, either he will not succeed to break out of the comfort zone, or he will surely fall back into his previous zone in some time. We need to learn to apply the first principle in our daily life. The first principle means a foundational assumption or understanding of something that can stand alone. In simple words, the first principle is the basic unit of an idea and which cannot be deduced from any other principle or assumption; it has to be unique and should work only for one or similar issue.

Most of the people we meet, regardless of their university degree, simply see the surface of the problems, or they may be able to see some superficial and deduced theory behind the cause. However, the real solution to the problem is hidden in the root cause that cannot be seen superficially. An intelligent person is that who manages to see a few steps behind and ahead of time. The present has the key of time; Past, and Future, because the present is the middle part of the journey in time. According to Einstein, the theory of relativity, time travel is possible when an object moves faster than the velocity of light.

It is the fact that to receive anything in life, we need to be worthy of it. Otherwise, things may come to us and leave with no time. Also, when we receive something that we do not deserve, we either dislike it or lose interest in it very quickly. If the frequency of things does not match yours, the vibration in which your every cell is vibrating will react uncomfortably, and then your mind produces an opposing frequency. As a result, either you get away from the attracted things, or things will slip away from the grasp of your midst. People often talk about getting out of one's comfort zone to face the greater challenges that promote our progress and growth. But getting out of the comfort zone is not as easy as it sounds; it's like diving into the ocean without learning to swim. There may be five out of a hundred who would survive drowning, but 95% would die because of lack of preparation. Getting out of the comfort zone means trying to reach a higher energy level or different state of mind, and if one does not know how to achieve such level, either he will not succeed to break out of the comfort zone, or he will surely fall back into his previous zone in some time. We need to learn to apply the first principle in our daily life. The first principle means a foundational assumption or understanding of something that can stand alone.

In simple words, the first principle is the basic unit of an idea and which cannot be deduced from any other principle or assumption; it has to be unique and should work only for one or similar issue. Most of the people we meet, regardless of their university degree, simply see the surface of the problems, or they may be able to see some superficial and deduced theory behind the cause. However, the real solution to the problem is hidden in the root cause that cannot be seen superficially. An intelligent person is that who manages to see a few steps behind and ahead of time. The present has the key of time; Past, and Future, because the present is the middle part of the journey in time. According to Einstein, the theory of relativity, time travel is possible when an object moves faster than the velocity of light. Let us suppose that time is an invisible river originating somewhere in the East and flowing towards the West. We all are floating on it and flowing towards the West. Let say the velocity of this river is 50 mph. If I manage to swim 70mph in the West direction, I will reach Future before anybody else swimming next to me. Similarly, if I swim with the same velocity but towards the East, I will reach the past, but in this case, I won't be able to see myself or somebody from my childhood because everyone flowed with the river. Thus, time cannot be a continuous series. It should be a discrete one; instead of flowing like a river, time should act as a photo album. We assume that all pictures from the past, present, and future are arranged chronologically in this thought experiment. These pictures are stored like CDs or DVDs in the time frame. This time, I would see myself and how the world was in the past or future. This also means that the future is already arranged in the album.

In the above thought experiment, one page of the album can be missing, and the future will still exist. But in the case of this time and river analogy, if the river is blocked for some time or a person is removed from the river, his future does not exist. If we have to believe in time travel, we will have to believe in photo album analogy more. If we consider the time as the entire photo album, each page represents the present time. The left side of the current page you picked is the past, and the right side is the future, and you can flip the page anytime you want. Visualize a small drawing book where you draw a person on the first page. On its second page, you draw the same person with different postures. You continued it until the last page; you give various posture to the picture. Finally, you flip the pages fast enough to see the motion of the picture. I used to draw a person doing a backflip when I was a kid. In this example, every current page determines the action of the upcoming page and the final outcome of the picture. This means every current page is important for the future. If the future is already there, then why should we work hard? We will get what we are designed to get, and the future is fixed. No, it's not.

The future is like the shadow of the present; if we change the shape today, the shape of tomorrow will be changed. Even though the future already exists, if it is so, everything beyond the present, towards the future, is mutable. Suppose I manage to travel in the future while writing this book right now, and I see myself being a famous and rich author 10 years from now who is living a perfect life with his wife and children. I return from time travel to the original time when I am writing this book, and I decide to change the future. I go outside, commit a serious crime, and got 10 years imprisonment. When I get out of jail, will I come out as a famous and rich author as I saw in time travel? Where are my children and wife? But I went to jail without getting married. If I time travel again 10 years back to the original time when I was writing this book and do time travel again, what would I see? In this case, you need to forget the imprisonment case because I am traveling to the time before committing a crime. If I travel 10 years ahead in the same you like last time while I am writing the book. The chances of me finding myself as a famous and rich author is high. By giving this example, I wanted to tell you that the future is the mirror image that mimics the present. If you want to change, add, or delete something from your life in the future, apply it to the present. Your present choice determines the future. Thus, by knowing the present well, the future can be imagined. It is like seeing one move of a chess piece and getting the future of the game. However, a single brilliant or dumb move of the piece cannot decide the win or loss of the game. Similarly, the more than average of what you do today will determine your future.

Beyond the doubt, there are so many methods, sources of information, and knowledge available in the market that claim to be effective ways to bring happiness to our life. But what makes them more effective is your action. If there is food on the table, you must perform eating (use hands and body system to engulf the food). Simply looking at the food and the table won't appease your hunger, neither will you get energy. Likewise, just collecting books for your home library does not make your mental library larger. Also, reading and knowing things do nothing until you actually carry out the information into the actions. Actions explain whether the knowledge you are acquiring will turn into fruition or not. Many people sell glitters for gold, but all glitters are not gold. All flowery sentences are good for physical ears, not necessarily equally well for our mental ears. You must be able to distinguish good from harmful.

When we try to bring changes, it is not necessary to change everything overnight. Change occurring step by step is more sustainable. The most important thing is completing what you started. Do not give up if you do not see the desired results out of this book in a couple of weeks. Instead, focus on your method, have faith in yourself, and be persistent on your goal. All the techniques discussed in this book are self-experienced and research-based exercises. If they are performed daily, the transformation is inexorable. I have lived with the principle of this book and have realized that we can receive anything we desire when we have extensive dedication. I managed to escape the adversity, ignorance, and infinite darkness of life with the principles discussed in this book and hope many struggling populations find this book as a small lamp to light their path out to the awareness, more towards the higher consciousness. As a human, the duty of us is to get oneself out of the misery first and then guide others towards the bright side of life. I have done my part, and the present is waiting for your action so that more people will be self-sufficient through you in the future. Let's unite together, learn from one another and break all limiting boundaries that have divided us into fragmentations. No one is inferior, and no effort is mediocre permanently. Everything in this world is mutable, so are we. Thus, wake up and get ready for the change; whether you are prepared for it or not, the change is impending.

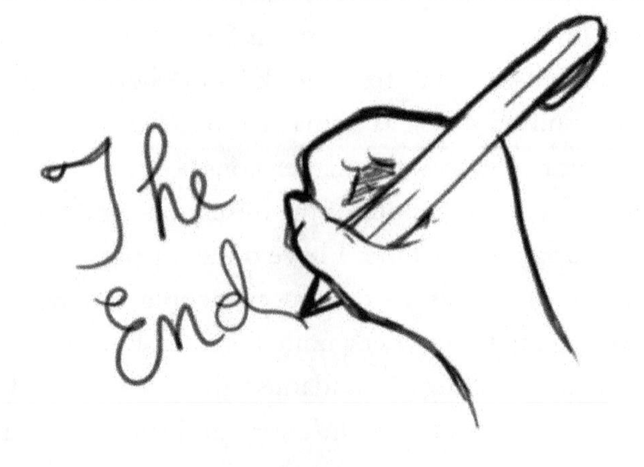

References

Sari, N. K. et al. (2017) 'The role of autosuggestion in geriatric patients' quality of life: a study on psycho-neuro-endocrine-immunology pathway', Social neuroscience, 12(5), pp. 551–559. doi: 10.1080/17470919.2016.1196243.

Saaresranta, T. and Polo, O. (2002) 'Hormones and Breathing', Chest, 122(6), pp. 2165–2182. doi: 10.1378/chest.122.6.2165.

Balasubramanian, S. (2016). Yogic breathing. Prana Science Institute.

Swami Prabhupada. (1972). Bhagavad Gita. The Bhaktivedanta Book Trust.

Stanhope, J. and Weinstein, P. (2020) 'The human health effects of singing bowls: A systematic review', Complementary Therapies in Medicine, 51. doi: 10.1016/j.ctim.2020.102412.

Kocaman, A. and Keles, O. (2019) 'Antibacterial Efficacy of Wire Arc Sprayed Copper Coatings Against Various Pathogens', Journal of Thermal Spray Technology, 28(3), p. 504. doi: 10.1007/s11666-018-0824-x.

de Toledo, F. W. et al. (2020) 'Unravelling the health effects of fasting: a long road from obesity treatment to healthy life span increase and improved cognition', ANNALS OF MEDICINE, 52(5), pp. 147–161. doi: 10.1080/07853890.2020.1770849.

Shashi Kiran et al. (2019) 'Effect of yogic colon cleansing (laghu sankhaprakshalana kriya) on bowel health in normal individuals', Yoga-Mimamsa, 51(1), pp. 26–30. doi: 10.4103/ym. ym_4_19.

DOW, C. (2019) 'Gut Feeling: Can microbes boost your mood?', Nutrition Action Health Letter, 46(7), pp. 8–10.

Do, K. and Yim, J. (2020) 'Effects of Muscle Strengthening around the Hip on Pain, Physical Function, and Gait in Elderly Patients with Total Knee Arthroplasty: A Randomized Controlled Trial', HEALTHCARE, 8(4). doi: 10.3390/healthcare8040489.

Fuentes-García, J. P. (1) et al. (no date) 'Chess players increase the theta power spectrum when the difficulty of the opponent increases: An EEG study', International Journal of Environmental Research and Public Health, 17(1). doi: 10.3390/ijerph17010046.

Bellew JW, Symons TB and Vandervoort AA (2005) 'Geriatric fitness: effects of aging and recommendations for exercise in older adults', Cardiopulmonary Physical Therapy Journal (American Physical Therapy Association, Cardiopulmonary Section), 16(1), pp. 20–31. doi: 10.1097/01823246-200516010-00005.

de Haan, T. and van Veldhuizen, R. (2015) 'Willpower depletion and framing effects', Journal of Economic Behavior and Organization, 117, pp. 47–61. doi: 10.1016/j.jebo.2015.06.002.

Tabei, S. et al. (2019) 'The effect of willpower workshop on anxiety, depression, and the excitement components in the students of Shiraz university of medical sciences', Journal of Family Medicine & Primary Care, 8(2), pp. 741–747. doi: 10.4103/jfmpc.jfmpc_406_18.

Nikmanesh, Z. and Mirkazehi, L. (2020) 'Research Paper: The Effectiveness of Positive Thinking Training in the Quality of Life and Emotion Regulation Among Patients with Multiple Sclerosis', Journal of Research & Health, 10(4), pp. 207–215. doi: 10.32598/JRH.10.4.363.7.

Baumann, K. et al. (2017) 'Commitment to Celibacy in German Catholic Priests: Its Relation to Religious Practices, Psychosomatic Health and Psychosocial Resources', Journal of Religion and Health,

56(2), pp. 649–668. doi: 10.1007/s10943-016-0313-9.
TED-Ed. (2016, August 11). How a single-celled organism almost wiped-out life on Earth [Video]. YouTube. https://www.youtube.com/watch?v=dO2xx-aeZ4w&t=81s

Chirumbolo, S. and Vella, A. (2021) 'Molecules, Information and the Origin of Life: What Is Next?', Molecules (Basel, Switzerland), 26(4). doi: 10.3390/molecules26041003.

de La Tour Simone and de La Tour Kevin (2011) 'Original Mind and Cosmic Consciousness in the Co-Creative Process', Frontiers of Philosophy in China, 6(1), pp. 57–74.

Eason, A. D. and Parris, B. A. (2019) 'Clinical applications of self-hypnosis: A systematic review and meta-analysis of randomized controlled trials', Psychology of Consciousness: Theory, Research, and Practice, 6(3), pp. 262–278. doi: 10.1037/cns0000173.

Fitzerald, L. (2004). The Mahabharat, Volume 7. Chicago, USA: The University of Chicago Press.

Spitzer, M. (no date) 'Stories and brain development: Reading aloud versus viewing videos', Nervenheilkunde, 38(7), pp. 496–498. doi: 10.1055/a-0883-3232.

Zhao, X. et al. (2021) 'Brain development from newborn to adolescence: Evaluation by neurite orientation dispersion and density imaging', Frontiers in Human Neuroscience, 15. doi: 10.3389/fnhum.2021.616132.

Voss, M. W. et al. (2019) 'Exercise and Hippocampal Memory Systems', Trends in Cognitive Sciences, 23(4), pp. 318–333. doi: 10.1016/j.tics.2019.01.006.

Weigmann, K. (2014) 'Why exercise is good for your brain: A closer look at the underlying mechanisms suggests that some sports, especially combined with mental activity, may be more effective than others', EMBO reports, 15(7), pp. 745–748. doi: 10.15252/embr.201439051.

Gould, E. (1998). Journal of college science teaching. New Brain Cells, 27(6), 376.

Nawaz, R., Nisar, H. and Voon, Y. V. (2018) 'The Effect of Music on Human Brain; Frequency Domain and Time Series Analysis Using Electroencephalogram', IEEE Access, Access, IEEE, 6, pp. 45191–45205. doi: 10.1109/ACCESS.2018.2855194.

Wu, J. et al. (2013) 'The effects of music on brain functional networks: A network analysis', Neuroscience, 250, pp. 49–59. doi: 10.1016/j.neuroscience.2013.06.021.

Haertl, K. L. (1) and Ero-Phillips, A. M. (2) (no date) 'The healing properties of writing for persons with mental health conditions', Arts and Health, 11(1), pp. 15–25. doi: 10.1080/17533015.2017.1413400.

Mantra-Tantra-Yantra Science. (2012, March 21). The sun rises in the west. https://siddhashram.blogspot.com/2012/03/sun-rises-in-west.html

Notes

CPSIA information can be obtained
at www.ICGtesting.com
Printed in the USA
BVHW051641260821
615314BV00012B/1112